July 28, 1991

Dear Mary,

Thank you so much for your gracious hospitality.

We look forward to your visiting us so that we can share with you some of the beautiful sights depicted in this book.

Love

Kathy, Alvin, & Rachel

II

"Wildlife: the best indicator of environmental quality. As long as the Atchafalaya maintains a healthy wildlife population, south Louisiana will be safe for all of us."

V

ATCHAFALAYA
America's Largest River Basin Swamp
C. C. LOCKWOOD

Published and for sale by:
CLAITOR'S PUBLISHING DIVISION
P.O. Box 3333
Baton Rouge, LA 70821
Phone 1-800-535-8141 (in LA (504)344-0476)

Manufactured in the United States of America

First printing Beauregard Press . . . . April 1981
Second printing Beauregard Press . . . . April 1982
Third printing Claitor's Publishing Division . . . . Nov. 1984
Fourth printing Claitor's Publishing Division . . . . May 1990

Graphic Design: Chet Boze
Printing: J.W. Moore Printing Co., Inc., Memphis, TN

CONTENTS

VIII

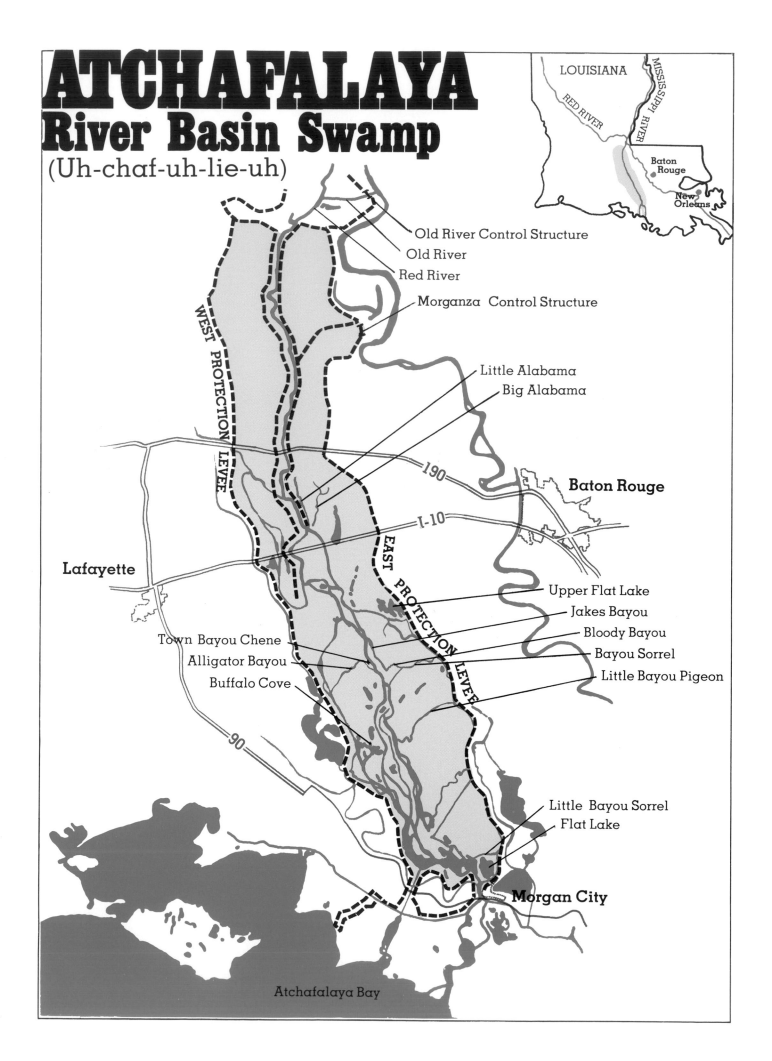

ATCHAFALAYA
River Basin Swamp
(Uh-chaf-uh-lie-uh)

LOUISIANA

RED RIVER

MISSISSIPPI RIVER

Baton Rouge

New Orleans

Old River Control Structure

Old River

Red River

Morganza Control Structure

WEST PROTECTION LEVEE

Little Alabama

Big Alabama

190

I-10

EAST PROTECTION LEVEE

Baton Rouge

Lafayette

Upper Flat Lake

Jakes Bayou

Bloody Bayou

Bayou Sorrel

Little Bayou Pigeon

Town Bayou Chene

Alligator Bayou

Buffalo Cove

90

Little Bayou Sorrel

Flat Lake

Morgan City

Atchafalaya Bay

1

INTRODUCTION

Winter is a brief time in the Atchafalaya. Almost as soon as the willow drops its last leaf the swamp red maples are dressing up their firey seeds and the yellow-tops cover the swamp floor with a tightly woven carpet of golden flowers. Today, though, is the real winter; cold, grey skies give no hue to the brown and leafless forest. The muddy current of Jakes Bayou is picking up volume and velocity with the January rains and waiting for help from the snow melt of the north to bring fresh water to the basin.

I take a break from reading over the journal I've kept of my experiences in the swamp during the past years, and gaze at the huge raindrops making craters in the silt-laden flow of fish-full waters. The pace of the storm quickens, and watching the pock-marked water from the stern window of my houseboat, *The Bayou Wanderer*, I think back to some of the other rainstorms I weathered out in canoes, bateaus, blinds, tents, and cypress stumps.

The rain pings as it hits my flat roof. It's a wonderful sound, one of nature's best. A deer hunter speeds by, the wake from his homemade aluminum bateau gently rocking the *Wanderer* from port to starboard. On his front seat lies an eight-point buck. To the rear, by the wooden windshield, is an old shotgun that is probably loaded with buck shot, some used lard tins that are probably filled with his dogs' food, and a red ice chest most probably filled with seven-ounce Miller beers.

The wooden windshield is painted red and green, reminiscent of old wooden bateaus. A few years ago such swamp chariots had to sport precisely these two colors to identify their occupant as a serious hunter, fisherman, or swamper. Now a new breed of bateaus, skiffs, and john boats ply the winding bayous of the basin, but the Cajun descendants steering them effortlessly through fallen trees and narrow bends are just as serious about their hunting and crawfishing.

When I'm exploring you might say I'm in Hog Heaven. If I come up to a small bayou, slough, or trail off my main course I can never resist trying it, and if my new trail splits I always again take the smaller one. I have this intense curiosity to see what is at the end of every bayou or what the view is from the top of a cypress tree: I dream of exploring some place before anyone else. Stories of explorers such as Lewis and Clark or LaSalle or Jedediah Smith always excited me. What a time they must have had seeing virgin territory! If I had the chance to go back in time and take one of their places I would seriously consider it.

The lifestyles of the swampers and the physical appearance of the swamp are changing somewhat with the times, but this great lowland still offers the same things that brought man to the basin in the first place . . . an abundance of natural resources.

To the Cajun it is his living: hunting, trapping, crawfishing, frogging, and crabbing. To the sportsman it is fishing for bass and hunting for ducks, squirrels, and deer. To the oil company engineer it is fossil fuels. To the timberman it is lumber. To the coastal fisherman it is a nursery for his catch. To the public it is a buffer zone where clean air and water exist. To the environmentalist it is North America's largest and last total swamp ecosystem.

What attracted me, at first, were the basin's amazingly abundant and diverse wildlife, its rookeries with thousands of egrets and herons, its waters with billions of crawfish, and its ridges with deer, squirrels, and woodcocks. Then the scenes caught my eye—the meandering bayous lined with baldcypress trees, the many glassine lakes reflecting vegetation into double images, and the mighty Atchafalaya River, the lifeline of the swamp. And then, finally, it was the people who engaged my attention— the colorful, interesting, friendly people who live, use, or think about the Atchafalaya Swamp.

Over the years I have come to care dearly for this great wetland and its inhabitants. It is a special place to me. It is a special place to Louisiana. It should be a special place to us all, for this 1.4 million-acre soggy Atchafalaya swampland has been giving itself to us unselfishly since the beginning of man.

WILDLIFE

"Just two hours left," I think to myself as I coast down the Whiskey Bay ramp of Interstate 10 and turn northward into the utter blackness of this moonless, muggy summer night. It will be a short span of time in which to cover fifteen miles of gravel road, two miles of jeep trail, a half-mile on foot to my canoe stashed in a back hole cypress swamp, and another two miles by water to my egret blind before first light.

The first twelve miles are the easiest as I rattle down the uneven road, occasionally hitting a deep rut or crossing a rivulet that jolts me as much as it does my old, worn jeep. At every bump I shoot a quick glance at my rusty Coleman ice chest transformed into a camera carrier, to make sure everything is safe. My high beams catch a doe nibbling the tender grasses near the roadside. The sound of my jeep's leaf springs hitting the frame startle her, and in an instant, white tail erect, she bounds into a smilax thicket. If only I could speed through the woods with her ease! One of my dreams. . . .

I begin to watch my odometer closely, for I know that two-tenths of a mile before the gravel road's end a jeep trail used only by deer hunters in the fall will be invisible on my right. The broomsage and dewberry completely hide the trail except in four places where sloughs cross it. The ruts are there, so by feel and memory I motor through the dark woods until I reach the first slough. Summer's low water levels in the swamps have dried it up somewhat. Of the four sloughs this is the worst. It doesn't look so bad this time. It's about forty feet across, with ruts in places two feet deep. The secret is to miss all previous ruts, be in low range, and zip across at twenty miles per hour. This way you are almost assured of not getting stuck, but you'll bounce your head off the ceiling of the truck at least two times . . . and I do. The next three sloughs are almost dry, and I am soon at the tall and crooked persimmon tree that marks the head of my trail.

From here, in two trips, I carry my paddles, cameras, tripod, food, water, and camping gear to my camouflaged canoe. As I prepare to paddle, push, and pole my favorite craft through the second-growth cypress forest, seeing traces of pink on the sparse wisps of clouds high in the summer sky, I know I will never make the blind for first light.

In a canoe, a good strong paddler can easily cover two miles in twenty minutes—in open water, that is. Here it is different. This is a back hole baldcypress swamp, the true swamp. Depending on the time of year, the water can flow eight feet deep or retreat, leaving two feet of soft mud. Today it is just above my knees and completely covered by water hyacinths, hydrocotles, and alligator weeds. If it were not for all the gear I carry I'd probably be better off trying to wade out to my blind, sticking close to the cypress trees where the ground is almost firm. The canoe is hard to push, pull, or shove through the aquatic vegetation, but a lifesaver when I have to cross open water above twenty-four inches of feet-sucking false bottom. More than once I have come home with clothes muddy enough to throw away.

Getting out to this area is very hard, and the colonial birds that nest here know it. That is why they choose this place. Man and animals alike find it difficult to disturb these birds' mating rituals and the raising of their young.

My canoe finally loaded and ready, I shove off with a green push pole. Squaaak! That's the first abrupt sound to break the constant chatter of the green tree frogs, and I see the silhouette of a yellow-crowned night heron weave through the cypress branches. Pushing hard, I cross many small lakes, drag through button-bush thickets, and pole under the towering cypress homes of Louisiana herons, anhingas, piliated woodpeckers, and barred owls.

As the morning glow increases, ahead I glimpse at last my destination: the island of cypress trees where my blind is located. The swamp canary—or prothonotary warbler—darts among the swamp privet shrubs singing its "sweet sweet" call.

A stranger could come within fifty feet of my blind and not see it. I can distinguish it only because I know it is there. This architectural wonder anchored to three baldcypress trees has been here for two and a half years and blends perfectly in color, if not shape, with its wild surroundings.

There is no geometric term for the shape of my blind, a cross between a triangle and a pentagon. Made of plywood, potato sacks, camouflage cloth, and Spanish moss, it is airy in the summer and cold in the winter. Carolina wrens have nested in it, and other creatures inhabit it at various times—with and without me. These fellow tenants include green anole lizards, tree frogs, raccoons, opossums, barred owls, yellow jacket wasps, mosquitos, numerous spiders, and large black ants. I come to see the wildlife, so I don't complain or even ask for rent.

At the blind I toss my gear up onto its floor, then hide my canoe in a nearby thicket. By the time I arrange my supplies, morning is here and the swamp is alive with the sounds of the day. There's the raucous thumping of the piliated woodpecker searching for grubs, the deep bellow of a bull alligator, and the continuous chirping of thousands of young egrets waiting for their first meal of the day. At least half the adult great egrets have gone in search of crawfish and other aquatic animals to feed their always-hungry offspring.

Because some of the nestling egrets are nearly the size of their parents, direct attention to those nests is unnecessary. The adult on guard sits atop a nearby cypress tree to watch and protect the young from hawks, raccoons and other predators. A few weeks earlier one parent would have always remained on the nest to shade the nearly naked chicks from the sun and wind. Now the young are doing everything but flying and would endlessly pester a parent on the nest for a regurgitated meal of fish caught from a nearby bayou.

Egrets nest together for protection, knowing that a hawk or raccoon would be too much for a single family. I once saw a red-shouldered hawk swoop down and land on a frog in the water hyacinths among the egret nests. Within seconds every nest had an adult bird squawking loudly in it with wings spread, head pointed down at the hawk. Then five egrets dove at the intruder and chased it away. The action provided quite a line of defense.

I steady my tripod and focus my long lens on a nearby nest. Three young egrets anxiously await their parents' arrival with food. Their heads sway as they survey the skyline, ignoring a passing pair of wood ducks, a green heron, and even a great egret. Then there is a tumultuous uproar as one parent arrives. The monotone chirping turns to adult-like squawks, and they jab and grab undauntedly at the big bird's beak. After a couple of good tugs, the feeding process begins. The parent regurgitates a sizeable, shad-like fish, then another and another, until she has dropped eleven into the waiting beaks of the three voracious young. The largest youngster gets seven of the eleven as my camera's motor-driven noise goes undetected in the feeding frenzy. Then, just as quickly as the parent came, she flies off to sit atop the cypress tree from which her mate has already departed to do his share of the fishing.

Three months ago I watched this same pair go through their courtship and nest-building rituals. Their particular small cypress tree ended up with two nests in it, just the same as last year. Other, larger trees in the rookery had up to ten nests apiece. When the courtship began the cypresses wore few leaves, but each was spectacularly adorned with one or more great egrets displaying fancy plume-like feathers grown only for this time of the year.

Other egrets trying to nest too close were rudely dismissed with viciously stabbing beaks—all a part of the ritual. Soon the invisible territorial lanes were established and nests were constructed—or to my way of thinking, thrown haphazardly on limbs of the rapidly greening cypress trees. It seemed as if a small breeze would destroy each and every nest, but most held up even through the violent summer thunderstorms, and many will remain in some form throughout the winter. Haphazard as they look, egret nests must be engineering marvels.

As the day passes, I eat some canned salmon, fruit cocktail, and crackers, and think of the real reason for my visit. Although I have been in this blind on thirty-six different days, I always came before sunrise and left before dark. Tonight I am going to camp here, up in this tree, and explore a back hole rookery at night. My hope is to get some photographs of mating frogs.

I have camped for many nights all over the Atchafalaya—in my tent, under my mosquito net, and even in my canoe when I was not close to dry land. This time is different because I don't plan on doing much sleeping. I want to see what happens in this area at night.

The day meanders as I watch a gator sun itself on a log matted firmly in place by the floating vegetation. A couple of little blue herons fish off the opposite end of the log, seeming nonchalant about the nearby gator.

I have seen gators in every one of the nine egret and heron rookeries I have explored in the Atchafalaya Basin. If they are alert, they can supplement their regular diet of fish, frogs, and nutria with eggs fallen from nests and with young, flightless birds. This one, though, seems content to sun himself on the log and leave the herons to themselves.

As the sun sets behind the darkening forest, I shoot a beautiful scene of an egret flying across the orange skies with the remnants of its breeding plume backlit against the setting sun.

On my ultralight camp stove I cook a couple of pork chops with potatoes and tomatoes. As the evening grows darker, the chorus of tree frogs intensifies. The cry of the nutria, so human sounding, the occasional squawk of a night heron, and the deep bellow of the alligator mix with the increasing croaks of the bull frog to entertain me during dinner. The mosquitos are not bad tonight, but I have my net just in case I need it for the few hours of sleep I will get later.

With supper down and the night dark as pitch, I know the time has come to set out. I pull my hipboots back on and wade over to the thicket hiding my canoe. Carefully, I stow my gear so that I can easily grasp what I need. My camera is rigged with 135mm lens and strobe to shoot gators or bull frogs. For the smaller green tree frog, my close-up unit is ready on the canoe floor.

I tie a rope from the bow of the canoe to the back belt loop in my Levis so I can drag the canoe behind and leave my hands unhindered to shoot pictures. Then I hook up my headlamp and gingerly scan the surrounding landscape. Eyes of red, green, and yellow light up everywhere. I am definitely not alone. Snakes and alligators have never bothered me in daylight hours, but now it is hard to take the first step. It's ten o'clock and pitch dark, and here I am, stuck in my tracks before I have even left the blind!

"Oh well, let's go. Most of those eyes probably belong to spiders. Alligators show two red eyes under flashlight, but luckily these are all single red eyes. Just spiders," I tell myself bravely.

After that first step, each successive one becomes easier. Then I stumble on a branch with a loose end, giving me a brief but heart-quickening scare as it pops up among the hyacinths. But soon sounds recede from my conscious attention and the life of the basin captures my thoughts.

I look and listen and absorb a new feeling for this swampland. Insects and frogs and even the egret nest become my subjects. As I wander aimlessly through the ponds and cypress ridges, time passes quickly. Remarkably, there is no sign yet of alligators or snakes, and therefore they no longer inspire fear. I still want to see them, but on my terms—which is to say, before they see me.

Hours later I finally find what I have come looking for: my headlamp beam illuminates hundreds of green tree frogs in one small area. Many, extending their throat sacks, are calling, and a few are mating. Quietly, I rein in my canoe, reach for the close-up camera, and begin my stalk.

To get the photograph I want, my camera has to be within two feet of my subject. So I put my beam of light on a mating pair and wade ever so slowly toward them. At four feet away the frogs part and jump.

I move even slower; but each frog seems to have this four-foot limit for a large strange creature with one bright white eye.

Then my luck seems to change. I am almost within four feet of a solitary male, and he is still calling undisturbed. My strobe is ready, my camera focused on two feet. Another step, and I will have my shot. The water six inches above my knee scarcely ripples, I move so slowly. The frog still sits in my lightbeam. I

am closer. Lowering my foot will put me within my chosen distance!

Then my rubber boot strikes something. "Oh, not another log! Will it scare the frog?" WHACK! A tail slaps my face. I fall backwards, instinctively grabbing my camera with my left hand and lifting it towards the sky as my right hand and both legs paddle me backwards to what I hope is safety. Ahead of me I can hear the splashes as the alligator submerges again and swims off.

Water gushes from my hipboots as I struggle to regain my balance. My left hand still holds my camera high and dry. Quickly I climb into the canoe, my heart pounding to the tune of the calling frogs and my mind trying to decide if I am still in good health. I am.

Safe; but enough is enough for one night. I empty my boots, hop back into the water and start towards my blind. Which way, though? I had been wading for over five hours looking only for animals and paying no attention to my route. "Why worry?," I must have thought earlier, for I have been in this rookery over thirty-six times and know most bird nests by sight. But that was in daylight. The cypress stands, the willow thickets, the tangles of button bush, and even the ponds all look the same tonight.

For two hours I wade from cypress island to cypress island. Finally, by using the stars to keep a straight line and making a sweeping semicircle about every 200 yards, I find my palace. What a relief to crawl under that mosquito net, eat my last few bites of fruit cocktail, and drift into dreams of alligators, crocodiles, Peter Pan and Captain Hook!

I awake a few hours later to the persistent buzzing of young egrets another day closer to fledging, the time when these young birds, along with the little blue herons, Louisiana herons, green herons, yellow--crowned night herons, cattle egrets, anhingas, wood ducks, Carolina wrens, and prothonotary warblers that I have personally seen nesting here, will soon spread out for the summer. It seems that these species alone would be enough wildlife for this one small area of the Atchafalaya Basin, but that is not so. This rookery begins to change as summer comes on.

And change it does. Each time I come back to this beautiful rookery there is a different kind of excitement and a different kind of scene. As June passes, the water under those great egret nests really drops. The wood ducks and their fully grown young are long gone to wetter areas. A few herons and egrets return to roost here each night, but nowhere near the thousands that are here in the February-June period.

August finds the hole almost mucky, with just a few inches of water and tight, ankle-grabbing mud. The frogs are still around, and dragonflies are everywhere. One day while slogging through this muck I caught sight of a green heron perched on an angular branch of a fallen willow and acting quite strangely. He kept lashing his head out at the sky. On closer inspection with my binoculars, I discovered that he was grabbing dragonflies out of the air. This was new to me, for I thought he would only eat fish. Later, upon researching green herons, I found that they do take advantage of abundant insect populations.

Summer is a quiet time in the swamp, and you rarely hear the far-off hum of an outboard motor. In a

season too late for crawfishermen and too early for squirrel hunters, swamp sounds consist mostly of the persistent buzzing of mosquitos mingled with the sweet songs of birds.

Still later, the rookery is invaded with a new dimension of wildlife: those like the deer, squirrels, coons, and others that favor land. October brings a few falling sycamore leaves and much dryer conditions. Real, solid ground materializes under the cypress trees. The sloughs and lakes are damp and mushy enough to envelop your ankles and are still mostly covered with the hardy, green water hyacinths, some of which are two feet tall. Only a few low spots in the lakes have eight to eighteen inches of water. Once, between two of them, I found a rut in the mud about eight inches deep with a clawed track on either side. Gator! I decided to investigate further and followed. A loud hiss startled me at the next lake, and there, looking like a log in the mud, was a nine-foot female gator with two six-inch babies on her head and ten or twelve others nearby making that unforgettable baby-gator sound. Ehhaaa!

I walked back to the hard ground of the tree line and then ventured deeper into this dry rookery. The cypress had yet to show any of its rusty autumn foliage.

At a pond well beyond another of my blinds, I saw a nutria feeding and quietly approached. With camera on tripod, I was lining up the shot when I heard a crash behind me. A white-tail buck leaped from a patch of button bush and crossed a dry lake just ahead of a doe. Before I could turn back to the nutria, a coon lumbered out of the hyacinths and crossed within a few feet behind me. It's not very often that you can see three wild mammals at the same time and spot. But the Atchafalaya is an amazing place. All total that day, I saw eight deer, five raccoons, a nutria, and seventeen species of birds.

One year I entered this rookery on January 14, at perhaps its loneliest time—not from the lack of wildlife, but for the cloudless feeling of completely overcast skies silhouetting the leafless baldcypress. Even the lowly water hyacinth had drooped and gone from waxy green to lifeless lumps of brown and white.

The nutria were still there and in renewed numbers, for there had been no sign of a trapper in this rookery.

Winter means, to the nutria's delight as well as the mink's and the otter's, that rains have been filling the ponds. Most hunting seasons are over, and the big buck deer can move out of their water-bound hiding places and return to the ridges where their favorite browse is abundant.

I walked over and, leaning on the stout, fluted base of a cypress tree, noticed two great egrets flying by. I wondered if they were just passing, or if that breeding urge was already beginning to blossom as they cruised the rookery. By placing my lips on the back of my hand and sucking air through the slight space, I made a squeaking sound that usually attracts song birds. Two Carolina chickadees came at me like divebombers, only to stop on a branch seven feet above my head. As I continued to squeak, they flitted around from branch to branch trying to find the intruder. Soon a bright red cardinal and a petite ruby-crowned kinglet joined the search. Finding nothing but this strange man making sounds with his hands, they soon lost interest and flew away.

Walking towards home, I saw two full-grown yellow-tops, an early spring flower, and the green leaves of many just sprouting. Soon they would make a yellow blanket through the woods. Closer to the edge of this pond, a maple showed its red flowers and seeds—maybe a little early for the real spring, but it would be here soon enough, and the cycle would be complete. The Atchafalaya Basin had survived another year, and man and animal alike were looking forward to a bumper crop of those tasty crustaceans, the red swamp crawfish.

I've told you a lot of tales about this little bald-cypress back hole rookery, but there is one more, and I can't leave this fine place without telling it. This happened right after I had built my blind near the egret nest. Marty Stouffer, a good friend and excellent filmmaker from Colorado, was down to help me make a film about the basin. We were going to the blind one afternoon to put all the heavy motion picture gear inside it and to blaze a trail through the water hyacinths. That way, we could come back more quickly and quietly the next morning.

Marty was taking his turn out front breaking the path, and I was behind slinging the hyacinths out of the way. The water was up to our chests, so we had taken off our hipboots and were wading barefoot when Marty said, "You know, Clyde, first couple of weeks down here I was kind of wary of the snakes and gators. Being up in the mountains for the last eight years, I kind of forgot about the old days in Arkansas."

I came back with, "Yeah, Marty, the snakes and gators don't bother me, but I am kind of unsure about those snapping turtles that are three and a half feet wide. Fact is, I saw a couple in here two weeks ago when I built this blind. One swam right under my canoe. They say a big snapper can break a broom handle like it was a match stick."

If any mortal man could walk on water, Marty sure approached the feat as he jumped back in our canoe. It took me the rest of the week just to get him to wade again.

Whether it be snapping turtles and woodpeckers or egrets and raccoons, I always see something when I come into this little rookery. I'd really hate to have to make a grand total of all the wildlife I've seen in this one area, and it's just a pinpoint compared to the whole basin. There are little areas like this scattered all over Louisiana's great swamp, and that's why people say that the animal life in the basin is amazing. Its multitudes in numbers are matched only by its diversity. In addition to over 300 species of birds that use the basin, there are at least 46 different mammals, 53 reptiles, 28 amphibians, and thousands of other lower forms.

To me, the fish life is particularly interesting. The waters of the basin house more than ninety different species of fish and in numbers or pounds one would find hard to add up.

To find out how many fish were out here, I checked with the Cooperative Fishery Research Unit at Louisiana State University, where a team of biologists was working on fish populations in the Atchafalaya. One group was taking "Fish Standing Crop Estimates" to see how many pounds of fish per acre were in the basin at selected sites. They invited me on one of their sampling trips.

It was a frosty November morning when we left the Bayou Pigeon landing for the Big Bayou Mallet area, but the rising sun warmed the day rapidly as it set the rusty brown cypress leaves aglow. Fall rains and early cold snaps had made the cypresses display their fall colors in a way I had never seen before.

When Dugan Sabins, the lead biologist of the field unit, stopped his Boston Whaler in a muddy old logging shoot and began unloading nets, I chuckled. This shallow slough would certainly not produce more than a few gar and goo fish.

After setting the nets 700 feet apart in this 50 foot wide and four-foot deep canal, the biologists put a 5 percent emulsifiable rotenone solution into the water. Rotenone is a chemical that lodges in the gills of fish, causing the gill capillaries to constrict, thus suffocating them.

I took this time to photograph some of the rusty-red cypress leaves that carpeted the bayou banks. Fifteen minutes later when I rejoined the biologists, the fish were already beginning to pop up. First the gizzard shad, a most fragile fish, emerged, and soon many others rose to the surface. I was amazed. One- to three-pound bass were everywhere, as were goggle-eyes, sacalait, and catfish. My chuckles turned to astonishment. I knew the Atchafalaya was full of fish, but never had I expected it to be like this.

Dugan said they missed some, especially the smaller ones that slipped through the net, but the 610 pounds of fish per acre that they did pick up proved my initial thoughts wrong.

When all the fish were up on the bank, the biologists classified, weighed, and measured each one. They came up with nineteen species in four main categories: 96 pounds per acre of sport fish, 387.8 pounds of commercial fish, 120.7 pounds of large predator fish, and 5.5 pounds of large forage fish. Dugan and his crew came back to the same place the next year and got 1,191.4 pounds of fish, and at another sampling site near Little Bayou Pigeon they took an average of 1,426 pounds of fish from one acre. Amazing.

I asked Dugan what would happen to the acre in which he had put the rotenone. He said the effects of the poison would wear off in a few days because of the cool water temperature and fish would begin utilizing

the area again shortly after that.

Dugan also told me, "The reason the Atchafalaya has so many fish per acre is because of the overflow water system. Take bass, for instance. They spawn in shallow water. In a lake or reservoir they must spawn near the shore where the eggs and fry are easy prey for other fish. In an overflow system like the Atchafalaya, the water can spread out through the woods, providing much more room to spawn and an abundance of hiding places and food for the young fish. Because of this we have a big crop of fish and they grow fast. Some bass in the basin reach a quarter pound and over six inches in length by the end of their first year."

Later I got the final tabulations for Dugan's study.

The fishery unit found in the lower basin, where a true overflow system exists, an average of 766.3 pounds of fish per acre as compared with 495.4 pounds per acre for a sampling site in the northern part of the basin that is now cut off from overflow. They also found that the lower basin had a higher percentage of sports and commercial fish and a greater overall diversity of fish. By contrast, in the upper basin one fish, the gizzard shad, was 51.3 percent of their catch.

They also compared their findings with similar studies in other bodies of water. I quote from their report:

> Fish standing crop estimates for the lower and upper Atchafalaya Basin were higher than most standing crop estimates reported in the literature. Lower basin estimates, in particular, stand out for their overall value and diversity. In an early study, Carlander (1955) reported average standing crop values of 256 pounds/acre for thirteen southern reservoirs, 398 pounds/acre for 27 midwestern reservoirs and 498 pounds/acre

for 10 natural river oxbows and backwaters (mostly from outside of Louisiana). All three values are lower than the average of 766.3 pounds/acre from the lower basin. Other studies report average fish standing crops of 341 pounds/acre from 42 Oklahoma ponds, (Jenkins, 1958), 358 pounds/acre from 22 Kentucky ponds, (Turner, 1960), 186 pounds/acre for 127 U.S. reservoirs (Jenkins, 1967), and 368.8 pounds/acre for 61 Corps of Engineers reservoirs (Leidy and Jenkins, 1977). The latter study reported the closest overall average standing crop to the lower basin average, 612.9 pounds/acre for 19 reservoirs in the Arkansas, White and Red River drainages. Of these 19, only four reservoirs had higher overall standing crops. None of the 127 reservoirs reported by Jenkins (1967) had a higher standing crop than the lower basin.

> Lower basin estimates were also consistently higher than others made in Louisiana waters. The 766.3 pounds/acre from the lower basin compares favorably with 201.5 pounds/acre from isolated Mississippi River oxbows (Lambolu, 1961), 362.1 pounds/acre from Spring Bayou backwater lakes (Lantz, 1970a), 262.4 pounds/acre from Cane River Lake (Geagan and Allen, 1960), 122.7 pounds/acre from Lac Des Allemands (Lantz, 1970b), 358.6 pounds/acre from Henderson Lake (Lantz, 1974) and 494.5 pounds/acre from the upper basin (this study).

From over 300 other water bodies sampled with the same methods, only four had a higher pounds-per-acre figure. And it should be pointed out here that most of the above-mentioned reservoirs are stocked with hatchery fish and managed by fisheries biologists, an expense of time and money. The Atchafalaya Basin with its overflow water regime is managed completely free of charge, naturally. Mother Nature does it for us.

Food is another reason for the abundant aquatic resources of the basin.

The red swamp crawfish, the white river crawfish, and some other smaller species of this crustacean are perhaps the most well-known members of the "feed" community. The approximately one hundred species of crawfish known to occur in the United States range in size from half an inch up to eight inches.

Louisiana has twenty-nine species, most of which are native to the Atchafalaya Basin. But the two most important are the red swamp crawfish, *Procambarus*

clarkii, and the white river crawfish *Procambarus acutus*, the only two species that are catchable in commercial pounds. Louisiana catches 99 percent of the nation's crawfish and consumes 85 percent within the state. Over 60 percent of the total catch comes from the Atchafalaya Basin.

Forty-two million pounds was the recorded catch in the basin in 1979 by commercial crawfishermen, not to mention all the crawfish that were caught by raccoons, night herons, egrets, large-mouth bass and hundreds of other creatures. It would be hard to estimate how many crawfish are out there in the peak time of the year.

Crawfish need a dry summer and fall so the ground can produce vegetation that gives young crawfish feed and hiding places. They need a winter with standing water and a spring rise with warmer waters. When this situation comes on just right, there will be a bumper crop of mudbugs, and this cycle is the rule in the Atchafalaya.

So each spring Saturday afternoon in Louisiana, many backyard chefs are preparing to put lots of salt, cayenne pepper, onions, lemons, and crab boil into a pot of water sitting on a butane burner, so they can have what we all cherish—a crawfish boil!

Personally, I like to sneak away from the Saturday party with about two pounds of boiled crawfish for my breakfast on Sunday morning. There is nothing quite like a crawfish omelet. First saute some finely chopped bell pepper and green onions in butter. Then add chopped tomatoes and the peeled crawfish tails.

When this mixture is hot, set it aside to whip up some eggs. (I beat the whites and yolks separately, and fold them together with salt and pepper just before putting the mixture in a black iron skillet with a light coat of butter.) As soon as the eggs take shape, add some finely grated cheddar cheese and then the crawfish mixture. Fold when firm and flip twice. Serve with fresh orange juice, and start your Sunday off right.

The crawfish may be the basin's most important feed species to man, but to swamp critters it is one among hundreds: the fry of bass, catfish, gaspergoo, goggle-eye, buffalo, choupique, and treadfin-shad; the tadpole of Fowler's toad, American toad, bullfrog, green tree frog, and spring peeper; the larvae of the mosquito, dragonfly, and millions of other little wigglers; the river shrimp, the phytoplankton, the zooplankton, and the leaf litter, the sediment, the crop of nuts, seeds, poms, drups, samaras, berries, and capsules. All these species make this swamp work in perfect unison with the rising and falling waters to feed the higher forms of life.

For example, let's take a look at the banks of a bayou throughout the year. During the high waters of spring, swamp privets, water elms, and dewberries hang their branches into the water. At this time you can see the broad-banded water snake sunning itself on the sturdier limbs. The prothonotary warbler sings as it flits from branch to branch eating little green caterpillars, and mockingbirds peck at the dewberries. Later in the summer deer come up to eat and hide in the fresh green materials that grow on the newly exposed bayou banks. As summer turns to fall and the water drops still lower, the muddy banks are exposed and the freshwater mussel is easy prey for the white ibis, who spent her spring and summer in the Atchafalaya marsh and bay. The raccoon also preys heartily on these small clams, and even I have boiled up a pot or two of these tough and chewy mollusks. With a sauce of butter and garlic, you'd think you were eating escargot—or at least chewing gum in a butter and garlic sauce. Now is also the time the fall grasses and flowers grow. They will soon be covered by the rising waters and make food and habitat for the crawfish, river shrimp, the fry of the catfish, and innumerable additional creatures.

So each year, in and out, the water goes up and down—some years more, others less. The crawfish will be affected in a good way one year and maybe negatively the next. But when the crawfish do poorly, the cottontail rabbit and whitetail deer do well. The water regulates a dynamic system that has the ability to bounce back quickly.

Only in an overflow swamp situation such as exists in the Atchafalaya can you have such attractive aquatic resources. Of all systems like this in North America today, the Atchafalaya is the largest and most important.

Some people have been saying for quite a while that the basin is silting up, choking the wildlife, and is not worth saving. Hogwash. The silt's a problem only if you want to keep the basin exactly unchanged. Nothing ever stays the same. True, silt affects wildlife, maybe even totally changing some habitats. But if the basin remains undeveloped, a wildlife community there—perhaps of a slightly different sort—will continue to thrive. Parts of the swamp may turn to bottomland and some of the marsh may turn to swamp, but between Highway 190 and Atchafalaya Bay we will still have a total overflow ecosystem, attractive and productive, for years to come.

Silt deposits from the Mississippi River created south Louisiana. Today this silt either drops off the continental shelf at the mouth of the Mississippi, because the Corps of Engineers has leveed and dredged the big river so much that its currents do not slow down or spread out enough to drop the silt sooner, or the silt enters the Atchafalaya Basin and spreads throughout the swamp and into the shallow Atchafalaya Bay.

Before 1973 this body of water was just a bay, but that year when we had a low tide and a north wind you could see exposed mud lumps. By 1975 they were exposed year-round, and in the summer of 1976 they had grown vegetation and were supporting nesting birds. Studies indicate that by the year 2000 we will have a substantial new marsh covering one hundred square miles in the Atchafalaya Bay, valuable new land for Louisiana.

Ducks have taken an immediate interest in this area. Louisiana Wildlife and Fisheries aerial surveys found few puddle ducks wintering in the Atchafalaya Bay before 1975. That year, with the new marsh lands popping up, researchers estimated over 35,000 ducks wintering in the new habitat. During mid December of 1976 over 100,000 puddle and diving ducks were estimated on Atchafalaya and Wax Lake deltas.

Mottled ducks, the only ducks that breed in Louisiana, began nesting there in 1976.

On an exploratory trip into the bay I observed eight of these ducks nesting; more interestingly, I found a single colony of least terns. The least tern, our smallest tern, nests in open areas on sand, silt, mud, or shells in colonial groups. Sometimes as few as four nests are found in one area or as many as fifty.

I first noticed the tern colony while walking across one of the new islands, slapping mosquitos as fast as I could. Those little buggers had found the new habitat also. From a distance I could see the petite terns flying almost swallow-like over a desolate-looking sandy space. As I approached, the terns began to dive at me, turning only a few inches from my head.

From their behavior I knew that I was in the middle of their nesting colony. Quickly, I surveyed the sand around me. No signs of nests. There were a few shallow depressions in the sand, as inconsequential as if they had been rearranged by the wind. If they were nests, perhaps it was just a little early for eggs. Then I found one—a single olive-tan egg flaked with dark-brown spots, blending perfectly with the sand.

The following day I returned with my portable blind, a square structure of aluminum conduit and brown double-knit cloth. The conduit is lightweight, and the double-knit clings to the blind so it does not blow in the breeze. My technique is to set it up out of sight of my subject and then, after getting inside and hanging my cameras and other gear on hooks, to creep forward hoping to look like an old tree stump. It worked with the terns.

After working my way slowly across the newly formed island, I found that the egg from yesterday now had a twin. Eight pairs of least terns were visible. One other pair had one egg. The rest were still in their courtship ritual.

My blind had inadvertently ended up eleven feet away from a courting pair—too close for my 500mm lens to focus on them. I had to back up a couple of feet. With my long lens on tripod and ready to shoot, I watched the male bring a small minnow to the vicinity of his mate. He flew over her a few times. She looked unconcerned. Then he landed near her, bobbing his head and flapping his wings like some well-dressed lady's man might do on the slick, strobe-lit plexiglass dance floor of a disco.

The female tern still paid him little attention. So he jumped on her back and began a little dance, offering the minnow to her by shaking it first on her left side and then her right. He would fly up, hover, then land again on her back. Finally she raised up, and they mated. Afterwards he flew about ten feet away with the minnow. Only then did she nonchalantly walk away from her nesting place, take the minnow, swallow it, and return to the nest.

About two weeks later I came back to find all eight nests with two or three eggs. Some of the fanfare between the male and female was still going on, but mainly they were concerned with incubating the eggs.

By my next trip to the island, a few of the eggs had hatched. The young birds, I assumed, were two or three days old—able to run well and to hide perfectly, for they blended with the sand just as the eggs had. The parents had quite a job feeding the young. I watched them bring an endless supply of small minnows to the rapidly growing youngsters.

In addition to the tern and the mottled duck, I also found nesting on these new islands the common gallinule, red-winged blackbird, common nighthawk, Wilson's plover, and killdeer. I found tracks of whitetail deer, bobcats, and otters. Wildlife can readily adapt to an area adjacent to an already abundant habitat. Just think of what a wildlife paradise this bay will be after it has more time to develop!

Another interesting experience in the Atchafalaya Bay involved a common tern. While exploring some new routes into the bay from a small bayou west of the Atchafalaya River, I came upon a large cypress log that had probably floated down the river and was now stuck in the shallow waters.

The log was about four feet thick and a good sixty feet long. A common tern sitting near the roots flew away as I approached. Seeing three eggs, I set up my blind on the opposite end of the log and waited for her to come back. After an hour, when it became apparent she would not return to her eggs while I was there, I left for awhile to think out a new strategy: I would set my tripod up in the water and hide behind my boat at a greater distance, using a longer lens and get the same shot. Picking a good position so the sun would shine nicely on the nest, I set up. By kneeling in the shallow water, which came halfway up my chest, I could use the boat as a blind.

It worked; the tern came back to her nest. But while I was looking through my lens with one eye, my other eye noticed some motion. Something was swimming around me. I stood up and the tern flushed. Fins were all around me. Sharks! I almost exclaimed aloud, "What are sharks doing in this freshwater bay?" As I climbed back in my boat, I decided to ask somebody else.

After counting all the fins, I determined there were eight small sharks circling me, each about three feet long. Too little to kill me, I suppose, but they were not going to have a chance.

Later I found out that during the summer and fall when the river is down, bull sharks, stingrays, anchovies, and other saltwater creatures have been found a good way up the river.

Aquatic creatures such as these have always interested me. I have seen and photographed them and many others while scuba diving in the deep blue waters of the Gulf. The Atchafalaya, too, offers many interesting aquatic animals, but generally its silt and nutrient-laden water is muddy, too much so to do any underwater photography. Occasionally, though, a backwater lake cut off from the river's overflow will drop all its silt and leave the water almost black-looking but clear enough to see through under water and to photograph.

The Blue Hole was one such place. This lake, almost a mile long and one fourth as wide, was once a part of Upper Grand River. It was cut off from the Atchafalaya River by the Corps of Engineers and now is landlocked except during the spring overflow.

Late one summer I decided to hike in and see if it was clear enough to get some underwater photographs of catfish and gar. A diving buddy of mine and I set out in a driving rain. My diving mask served as an excellent windshield as we motored toward Upper

Grand River from Ramah. The rain felt good on a warm day.

We parked my boat near a little slough that goes into the lake during high water. At the time, it was four feet up the bank. "Good," I thought. "No muddy water has gotten in here for awhile."

In a small pack I carried my mask, fins, and snorkle. Phil and I hiked half a mile to a little pond where we noticed a slide down the muddy bank. I made a mental note to come back and photograph the otters that use the slide.

On the other side of the pond another dry slough led the way to the Blue Hole. As we got closer, water began to trickle through it. Muddy water. Phil remarked that if this were muddy, the lake probably would be, too. I agreed, but we went on anyway.

A green heron flushed and flew down the waterway ahead of us. Snakes and frogs slid or jumped into the water as we intruded on their afternoon. As the slough widened, I told Phil that we were almost there.

We looked at the lake with disappointment; it was muddy. Still, I put on my mask, fins, and snorkle and swam out, hoping to find clearer water away from the slough. Phil sat on the bank. With only my snorkle sticking above the water, I kicked my way toward the center of the lake. At first I couldn't see my hand in front of my face, and visibility didn't improve beyond. No good, even for close-up photography.

Partially disappointed that the water was murky, but feeling good to be swimming in its warmth after the hike, I looked up to get my bearings. Right in front of me was a nine-foot alligator! It was staring at me from only thirty feet away. Phil, 400 yards away, was waving his arms frantically. Glancing back at the gator, I decided to get out of there as fast as I could!

My first kick was so ferocious I got a cramp in my right leg. Noticing that the gator had submerged only scared me more. With my hands and one leg, I swam about a hundred yards. Stopping to massage my cramp I saw that the gator had resurfaced a hundred yards in the other direction. "Huh," I thought, "it's scared of me, too!"

At ease, I swam casually back to Phil at the mouth of the slough. I guess my slow movements appeased the alligator, for soon, he began to follow me.

When I got to shore I asked Phil why he didn't warn me of the alligator. He said he was trying to, but my ears were underwater and I couldn't hear him.

Our friend was now a hundred yards offshore and

eyeing us. Once ashore I regained some courage, so I decided to swim out a little way and see how close I could coax the gator. Phil hid among the bushes, and I swam out. Maybe he or she would think I was another gator. "Ehaaa, ehaaa," I called, trying to imitate a baby alligator's sound. The gator came closer. A curious ritual developed. Slowly she would sink underwater, and I would immediately panic and swim for shore. This went on time after time, until I had finally gotten her within ten feet of me and only twenty-five feet from shore. Nothing better on a rainy afternoon than a game of alligator tag!

Hiking out through the muddy slough, content that we had experienced our share of excitement for the day, we heard a shrill, "Kee-you! Kee-you!" as a red-shouldered hawk flew over us, close to the tree tops.

This hawk, *Buteo lineatus*, is the most common bird of prey in the basin. It prefers the dense, wet woods where snakes, frogs, and fish are easy to find. A pair's flight during their courtship ritual is another of the basin's animal dramas.

I first saw this display in early February on a warm sunny day during my first year in the Atchafalaya. The male hawk called repeatedly as he circled high into the sky. I tied the stern rope of my canoe to a cypress knee and watched him climb higher and higher. The female flew across the bayou and landed on a high branch. Then the male dropped suddenly, like a rock falling out of the sky, and swooped over her. She rose to fly with him for a few minutes before landing in the woods. As the male climbed and dropped, over and over, they gradually moved farther into the woods and out of sight. I assume they mated over the next few days and began to build their nest.

I decided that day I needed to find a red-shouldered hawk's nest and photograph it; but that goal eluded me, for these hawks usually pick a secluded place way back in the swamp. Then one day a few years later I was fishing with Ben Skerrett in Little Bayou Gravenburg. We had been in the area of Gravenburg, Buffalo Cove, and the Si-bon Canal since before dawn. It was a sunny day in early May and I was intensely watching the fresh, green swamp. While looking for a great landscape photo I saw a red-shouldered hawk circling above, calling at us in a manner that convinced me we were near her nest. I asked Ben to stop the boat. No sooner than he did, I saw a second hawk, carrying a three-foot snake, fly low among the cypress trees and swoop to a nest-like structure.

Immediately, the heads of three young stuck up over the edge of the nest as they began to fight for their share of the food. Excitement ran through my veins. I told Ben I'd be back in a couple of days with materials for a blind. I hoped to build one in an adjacent cypress tree and get some photographs of the parents feeding the young birds.

Six days later I returned to try my plan. I tied up to a nearby cypress and looked eighty feet up to a fork that might support my blind. Thirty feet over and eighty feet up I could see the three nearly full-grown young hawks peering over the edge of the nest at me as I filled my pack with hammer, nails, rope, cameras, tripod, electrical remote release, film, water, and camouflage cloth. Finally I strapped a couple of two-by-fours and a small piece of plywood on my back. The pack weighed close to fifty pounds and I had great difficulty making my way to the first limbs. Halfway up the tree I was tired and sweating

profusely; my jeans and long-sleeved shirt were too much clothing for this hot day. The birds still peered over the edge of the three-foot-wide nest.

On the verge of exhaustion, just as I finally made it to the level where I could see into the interior of the nest, one of the parent birds flew over, calling to the young. In single file each of the almost fully feathered birds leaped off the edge, spread its wings, and flew away to a nearby tree. It was their day to leave.

"Well, you win some and you lose some," I thought as I climbed on up so I could at least photograph their nest, in which lay half of a broad-banded water snake.

On the boat ride home I consoled myself with hopes for the following year, for a lot of hawks use the same nest year after year. At home, I looked up the red-shouldered hawk in Bent's *Life History of Birds of Prey* and found out that this species of hawk does use the same nest often but sometimes skips a year and moves nearby. I also learned that the adults build or repair the nest for about twenty-eight days, incubate the eggs for about twenty-eight days, and drive the young hawks from the nest before thirty-six days. So I figured if I came back here ninety-two days before May 9 next year I could see some nesting activities, build my blind, and have a captive audience of a mother bird feeding some young ones that couldn't fly. How wrong I was.

The next February when I came back there were no signs of hawks anywhere. Had they been shot? Had they moved? I didn't know. A week later I checked again: still no sign. In the first week of March, while on a three-day camping trip, I again passed by: no hawks. I climbed their tree and saw no sign of nest improvement. I decided that they must have chosen another site that year.

Disappointed, but still glad to be in the woods for a few days, I moved on out Little Gravenburg into Big Gravenburg and later into Buffalo Cove, where I stayed for a beautiful sunset and then camped on the banks of Fausse Point Cut.

The following day I traveled on up the cut into Alligator Bayou, Bayou Chene, across the Atchafalaya River, up Tensas Cut and down upper Grand River, and then spent the rest of the day exploring the East Fork of Bayou Pigeon.

The water was high in these woods, so exploring was easy and I was having a good day just for the fact of seeing some country that I hadn't seen before. As I was noticing what a fine crop of dewberries was growing along this canal bank, and wondering if Calvin Voisin had picked any for wine making, a hawk flushed out of a tall baldcypress tree. Not only was she a red-shouldered hawk, but also I could easily see a nest in the nearly naked tree. She flew about 300 yards to one of the old red cypress giants left years ago by the clear-cutters because it was hollow. Its top branches stuck fifty feet above the swamp woods canopy. Up above, circling and calling loudly, was the male hawk. Because I was intruding on their territory, I hurried to complete my survey.

At the bank I tied my boat and forced my way through the dewberry thicket. The nest was not as big as the one on Gravenburg, probably meaning it had just been built that year. It was in a big tree, and the only other tree as tall was sixteen feet away—sturdy enough for a small blind, but maybe too close. Quickly I skimmied up; at eighty feet I sat in a three-branch fork and looked slightly down at the nest. One egg—yea! Each of the three branches was less than four inches in diameter, and I was swaying with the wind about three feet to the south, then back six feet to the north. Before leaving, I measured in my mind the dimensions and design of a small blind. Seven days later I came back with six short pieces of two-by-fours and an eighteen-inch by thirty-inch piece of sturdy plywood. After quickly nailing these into position I stapled camouflage cloth around the sides and top.

I waited almost a month before returning, to allow the birds to accept the blind and the cypress leaves to come out around it. Then one morning about 4:30 I paddled a pirogue up to the flooded bank near the nest and quietly waded up to the blind tree. The water had risen to cover the bank and was three feet deep under the nest tree. Halfway up the tree I heard the parent bird leave. Once in the blind I crossed my legs, cut a slit in the camouflage cloth, put my camera on a small unipod and waited patiently for daylight. The young hawk was just barely covered with down. As the sun rose I could hear both parents yelling "Kee-you! Kee-you!" nearby. When by 8:30 neither had returned to the nest, I left. The nestling was too young to be left alone any longer.

A few days later I came back in the same manner, but this time I brought some black cloth to put on the inside of the camouflage cloth to ensure that the hawks could not see me. The young hawk had grown, so I stayed until 9:30. Still, neither parent returned to the nest.

The next week I returned with no better luck. So on

my fourth trip I again worked on my blind, adding two more layers of cloth to make it more soundproof and a sound barney (a cover for a camera to muffle its clicking sound) for my Nikon.

On May 2, I made my fifth try. The water was already leaving the woods. Summer was almost here. The young bird was beginning to look like a real hawk. I was surprised and encouraged that one of the adults returned before sunrise, called six times, and left. My blind improvements must have done some good. But it was too dark to get a good picture, so I waited until 1:30 that afternoon. When she did not come I left, not knowing what to try next.

Ten days later I returned to try an evening. Maybe the parents would come back to the nest more readily in the late afternoon. They didn't. I made camp about a mile down the canal and planned for the next morning to be the last in the blind.

At 4 A.M. as I went in, the adult bird flushed as usual. At sunrise I got some nice photos of the young hawk flapping his wings, so I knew that any day now he could leave. By 10:30 the parents had not returned and I finally had to admit to myself that this blind was just too close. My last resort and only alternative was to set up a remote control camera. I did, taking a hundred-foot spool of wire down to the now dry ground below the nest. At 11:15 I was lying on the ground completely covered with leaves except for a small piece of see-through camo-cloth over my face. In one hand was a switch to turn my motor-driven camera and in the other a desire to slap the mosquitos and ants crawling all over my body. I resisted, suffering through the insect torment as I watched the nest. The minutes passed into hours. I could see a bird circling overhead, but none near the nest. I remained motionless, except for a contorted movement of my lips to try to get a puff of breath to knock down an assaulting mosquito.

Then my efforts and hard work were rewarded. Like a flash, she swooped through the trees, lower than the nest. She had a frog in her mouth. Spreading her wings, she glided up to the nest.

Once she landed, I hit the switch. Ker-whack, ker-whack, ker-whack, the motor drive spoke six times. The hawk dropped the frog and left. I finally had a sequence of photographs of the red-shouldered hawk.

After taking my equipment down I left, giving my wishes that the young hawk would fly high and live well among the other wild creatures of the Atchafalaya Basin.

Once, while telling Alciede Verret, an old swamper who lives near the Atchafalaya River, that I was looking for a hawk's nest, he said, "You know, a hawk will only eat a naked lizard." He claimed that while out hoeing his turnips one day he saw a hawk land on a dead limb with a lizard in its claw. He said that the hawk proceeded to pull all the skin off that lizard before he ate it. The four men sitting on Alciede's porch drinking coffee just nodded in agreement and waited to put in their two cents. The bull sessions are famous on Alciede's porch. The company is always good and the coffee hot.

My last visit with Alciede was one of those typical bull sessions.

14

SWAMPERS

Setting my outboard in reverse as I approach an empty spot on the thirty-foot cypress log dock, I see two black cats and a Heinz 57 dog jump (as if they were caught redhanded) out of some visitor's boat. As I tie and walk up the steep bank, a couple of heads peer over. Alciede booms to his guest, "Oh, that's just Lockwood. He's staying out here now," and then to me, "Come on up here. My generator won't quit leaking." Alciede's nephew Moose, a tugboat pilot, is hard at work on the leaking bowl sans filter and the gas line of an ancient Kohler gas generator. Alciede is saying one thing; Walter, his brother, is contradicting him, and John Stockstill stands nearby agreeing with neither. Moose and his friend just grin and do what they know will fix the old contraption.

Stories are passed. Walter says, "You want to know about a guy that really roughed it out here? I remember when we stopped at an old lean-to along the river where Robert Frejou lived—boy, it was primitive. We went in to warm up and get some coffee. He was crouched under the smoke that rose from his unvented woodstove. 'Come on in,' he said, 'but duck down under the smoke.' "

John adds, "Yeah, I remember that fellow was black from all the soot, but he was happy as could be—you'da thought he was in the Hilton."

Alciede chimes in, "Well, what we doing out here when we could be on the porch drinkin' coffee and shootin' the bull?"

John interrupts with, "Well, Alciede, I shot all the bull I got. If I'da knowed we were going to the porch I'da saved it."

I glance around Alciede's kitchen while the others move to the porch. I see six kinds of store-bought cookies sitting next to his famous bread pudding, a Hawaiian upside-down cake, a pink cake with chocolate icing, and a pot of rice. Next to a head of cauliflower and two turnips as big as volleyballs is what is left of last night's deer ribs and turnip stew (which I taste and find delicious). The fare is meager picking, according to Alciede, who proclaims, "Between running my traps, trying to get my brother back to Herbert's bayou, and fixing the generator, I hadn't had time to cook a thing."

Two more boatloads pull in, one carrying a fellow who had sunk a boat at the edge of the river last week. Alciede had told him they better be glad they were close to shore because right off that point it is eighty-five feet deep. Sure enough, the first thing they say when they come in is that the depth finder they brought showed the water to be exactly eighty-five feet deep.

Alciede has been in this basin for almost all his life, and you'll soon see through all his tall tales and general bulling around that he does really know the Atchafalaya Basin. You could almost say he has been to every spot and has a tale about each place.

Alciede moves to the kitchen to fix the coffee while John asks openly if anyone knows where Frog Lake is. Alciede immediately comes back. "Do I know where Frog Lake is! It's just back of Brison. Fact is, I was lost there once. Got greedy—I was catching so many fish that I went out to bait my lines twice. In the dark I got turned around and only found my way back by a lightning storm. Every time it would flash I'd get my bearing and move on. When I got back to the camp at 11 P.M. Agricole Theriot was playing the fiddle with my brother and some others cheering him on. They hadn't even missed me."

Skipper Verret, a distant relative of Alciede's who just arrived, asks how Alciede's stomach is doing. Alciede barks back, "Stomach, nothing wrong with my stomach. Fact is I can eat anything I want. It's better than it was when I was twenty-seven."

Skipper is referring to Alciede's recent kidney stone operation. The old man of the swamp spent about eighteen days in the hospital, his longest absence from the swamp in many years. He was seventy-nine years old three weeks ago.

'Cide goes on, "Ain't nothing wrong with me but my left knee and it can't be fixed. I almost thought about going ahead and getting a peg leg."

John chimes in, "Go ahead, 'Cide; if it works I'll get one too."

Skipper says he will loan 'Cide a pair of crutches, and Alciede blows up. "Crutches, I can't trap with crutches! Why, I'd bog down in the lilies."

The conversation could go on forever, so I make my excuses and head for the boat—but not before Alciede gives me a big head of cauliflower to drop off at Calvin and Gwen's.

Gwen Carpenter summed Alciede up beautifully in an article she wrote about him. It goes like this:

He speaks of dogs so lazy they have to prop against the fence to bark; peppers so hot you just pass them over the pot instead of putting them in the food; shrimp so plentiful you dip them from the bayou with a straw hat; the river falling so fast you have to run to get a drink of water; bayous so muddy you can get bricks from them; and fish biting so good you can bait with plastic.

He cooks two pounds of dried red beans, a gumbo with twelve squirrels, two dozen home-made rolls, a gallon of potato salad and a twenty-inch bread pudding on a Wednesday when no visitors are expected. If it were Sunday, or if company was coming, he would cook more.

He eats two dozen flapjacks, a stick of butter and a pint of fig preserves to accompany a quart of milk as a bedtime snack.

He wades, paddles, and poles his way through twelve miles of knee-deep slush with his seventy-five-pound pirogue loaded down with raccoons, mink, nutria and otters. His only complaint? The ice is damaging his pirogue.

He grows mustard greens big as dishpans, parsley that has to be mowed with a lawn mower, figs so large that three of them will fill up a quart jar, and a sweet potato three feet long.

Alciede Verret is only seventy-eight years old. What will he be like when he's one hundred? In South Louisiana it's common for an old man to make a living by trapping and fishing in the swamp where he was raised. Surrounded by his crowd of dogs and cats, he makes fish nets, cuts firewood for his stove, launders on a scrub board, and blasts rabbits out of his garden from his back porch as swampers have done for generations. But that is where the similarity ends.

Instead of living for months at a time in seclusion as proper hermits do, this old gentleman entertains as many as twenty people a day. Instead of living on boiled opossum, or whatever swampers are supposed to eat, Alciede cooks a banquet every day. His dishes have won numerous awards and his culinary skills were even featured on a television program.

But it's his personality that really sets Alciede apart from the stereotypical hermit of dour disposition greeting unexpected guests with a scowl and a shotgun. "Ya'll get out!" he booms, without even checking to see who has just landed at his dock. By the time the visitors have climbed the river bank to his house, the coffee water is on the fire and Alciede is standing in the doorway beaming as if he hasn't seen another human being in a month. This may be his fifth pot of coffee and seventh set of visitors for the morning but they will never know it from the welcome they receive.

They may have interrupted the mending of a net, the painting of a boat, or hoeing in the garden, but he assures them he was just getting ready to take a break and make a fresh pot. Perhaps they are total strangers looking for a good fishing hole. Such minor details make no difference to Alciede's hospitality, which is dished out generously with his coffee and conversation. One thing is certain. Once someone has found his way to Alciede's kitchen, he will always come back.

An endless stream of fishermen, hunters, surveyors, writers, photographers, explorers, scientists, lawyers and outlaws make their way through the swampy wilderness to his ever open door. "It looked like the blessing of the fleet this morning!" he blusters as he nods his head in the direction of the boat dock. "They ran out of places to tie up and just started tying to each other. If one bow line had broken, fourteen boats would have drifted off." When his niece suggests he needs a closet for his coffee cups, he sputters, "Nonsense, they stay in circulation too much to need a resting place."

Along with the gallons of coffee served every week, there are always platters of homemade fig bars, pumpkin turnovers big as dinner plates, twenty pounds of fruit cake, three pans of wild honey cake, five pounds of chocolate fudge, or maybe just his $7 bread pudding. This famous concoction starts with a loaf of stale bread to which he adds pure cream, eggs, butter, sugar, raisins, and pecans. Then each serving is smothered in a rich white rum sauce. It took the name "$7 bread pudding" when Alciede's social security check was increased by that amount. "Hummph," he snorted, "that will only pay for one of my bread puddings!"

Everything else about Alciede is as extravagant as his bread pudding. He hurtles headlong into life and embraces it with both arms. In the fall, when other gardeners are planting their quarter-ounce packs of turnip seeds, Alciede sows a whole pound. Come spring, when fishermen put out twenty-five to thirty hooks just to see if the fish are biting, Alciede puts out 200.

16

When his wife died, Alciede consoled himself with whiskey, as men have done for centuries. But, not being a person to do things halfway, Alciede stayed drunk for ten years! Eventually, he realized he was drinking a fifth of whiskey each day without even getting tipsy. He poured out his last bottle and has not touched whiskey since. "I was afraid I might become an alcoholic," he grins.

Several years ago, a butane refrigerator exploded in his face as he tried to light it. The doctors said he would never live. He said, "Hogwash!" When they said he would never walk again, he said, "You just watch me," and stalked off with one leg shorter than the other. When they said his head would never grow hair again, he just "Hummphed." He "Hummphs" again today as he tells the story and runs his hand through his thick white curls.

The stories flow out endlessly. Some are startling or funny in their own right, but many are entertaining simply because of the vivid language in which they are told. They provide respite from the routine of whatever life the visitor has temporarily left behind in civilization. People who would ordinarily never meet become acquainted while sitting on Alciede's porch or around his wood stove. A businessman forgets the contract he lost yesterday, a construction worker forgets the lack of jobs at his union hall, and a local outlaw forgets his upcoming trial as they all escape together into an account of the death of Pancho.

Assuming an expression on his face suitable for such a topic, Alciede launches into the tale. Peter Bunch, another swamper and Alciede's lifelong friend, owned an elderly beagle named Pancho. Pancho was notorious for raiding the boats of visitors while they were up the hill visiting with Pete. He was especially fond of bread and left many a traveler with plain baloney for lunch. Each time it happened, Pete would feign surprise that his dog would do such a thing. Pancho, trying to look innocent despite the crumbs on his muzzle, would thump his tail on the ground and burp. Over the years, Pancho's thieving habits netted hundreds of loaves of bread for himself and many good laughs for Peter Bunch.

One afternoon, Alciede was returning from town with a boatload of groceries. He had passed a couple of hours visiting on Pete's porch when suddenly he jumped up and exclaimed, "Oh, no, Pete—I've killed your dog!" "How do you mean?" replied the puzzled Pete, who is as unflappable as Alciede is excitable. "Well, old man," Alciede continued, "he just ate a whole pack of raw yeast rolls from my boat. Now he's gone and drunk a lot of water and he's lying in the sun. When that dough starts to raise it'll be the end of him for sure!" Old man Bunch peered down at the contented Pancho dozing in the sun and said he doubted it. But the next morning he discovered the ancient hound had passed away in his sleep. To this day, Alciede insists that he inadvertently caused the death of Pancho.

One of my favorite stories concerns Alciede's cousin, Albert Verret, who was employed as a cook for a lumber camp during the 1920's. Such camps were large house boats where the timbermen lived while cutting down the huge cypress trees deep in the swamp. Every night after supper, Albert would take all of the dishes outside to the deck of the campboat, where he would wash and rinse them in the river before bringing them back indoors to dry.

An incurable sleepwalker since childhood, Albert would frequently scare the daylights out of his companions by strolling around the camp in his sleep. One freezing cold night he got out of bed and, still sleeping, collected the entire supply of dishes and carried them to the deck as if to wash them. Once outside, he walked right on overboard, carrying his load of dishes to the bottom of the icy waters. The dishes made such a clatter that by the time Albert popped up, the population of the whole camp was awake and standing on the deck, ready to rescue him. The men were left with not even one dish from which to eat, but Albert was finally cured of sleepwalking.

That's what they come seeking—not the coffee and rich food but the even richer companionship of a man who has never seen a humdrum day. Nothing average ever happens to Alciede. He lives at an intensity that would exhaust other people. Healthier than men half his age, he can paddle a pirogue or swing an axe all day without ever getting out of breath enough to stop talking. Two years ago, a local fisherman noticed Alciede attempting to maneuver a twenty-five-gallon butane bottle to the top of the fifteen-foot river bank. He stopped to help and was greeted by: "When a seventy-six-year-old man can't handle a 200-pound bottle by himself, it's time to give up," and Alciede went right on up the hill with his burden.

However, just like everything he does, when Alciede gets sick he is sicker than anyone else. Describing an attack of the flu, he thunders, "Sick! Old man, I guess I was sick! St. Peter had the key in his hand but he put it back in his pocket at the last minute." From the looks of things, St. Peter will keep that key in his pocket for many years to come.

Gwen Carpenter is certainly right about Alciede's never doing anything halfway. I found that out again when I went to check trot lines with Calvin Voisin. Calvin, by putting out a few hooks a day, over a week's period finally had 150. Alciede started with 200, as usual.

The morning that I joined them to see what they were catching was one of those few clear but icy winter mornings that will make your fingers numb. Their hooks were in the cove, which is just about midway between where the two live. We took a short bateau ride which brought us to a ridge.

Carrying paddles and fish buckets we crossed the ridge, kicked the ice out of two hidden pirogues, and paddled out through a trail of dead hyacinths. Calvin and I were in an old black pirogue and Alciede was by himself in the other. The wind at our back blew us

17

toward the lake. Alciede said, "That's quite a wind. It's no use to check your lines on this side. They won't bite. On the other side out of the wind you'll catch a bunch."

Sure enough, as Calvin and I struggled with wind and checked line after line, all we caught were ten polywogs. The polywog is better known as the yellow bullhead to most people outside the swamp. It is quite tasty when fried up fresh, but it only brings fifteen cents per pound to the fisherman, hardly worth the effort to carry it to the buyer. What Calvin wanted was big blue catfish.

We crossed the now white-capping lake and had three more lines to check. Bingo! The lines out of the wind had twenty-five dollars' worth of blue catfish on them.

It was a struggle crossing the lake against the wind with a boatload of fish and two men in a one-man pirogue, but the lake was beautiful and the hard paddling kept us warm. Still, our fingers were numb and feet wet as the waves put six inches of water into the boat. At the starting point Alciede was back with about the same amount of fish.

I asked Alciede to describe the biggest fish he had ever caught. His eyes lighted up as he said, "Some years ago I caught a sixty-six-pound blue catfish. Got it on a snag line." When I asked what he did with it he quipped, "Sold it, of course."

Sitting on the bank sorting the fish, we watched as a group of fifty mallards settled back down on the far side of the cove. We had flushed them up earlier.

Later that day Calvin and Alciede went to Bayou Sorrel to sell their fish—one of the few reasons they ever leave the middle of the swamp.

Calvin lives with Gwen about two miles from Alciede's house. They are some of the few who still live full time in the swamp, and the only ones still in their youth. Most of the rugged group who refuse to accept the luxuries of proper civilization are old men. It wasn't always like this, though.

Before 1927 there were quite a few swamp folk. Communities such as Bayou Chene had churches, stores, sugar mills, and many homes. Alciede and others have fond memories of life in that community. But these folks were chased out by the 1927 flood and told by the Corps of Engineers they could expect higher annual floods once the east and west protection levees were put up. Some stayed in floating campboats, but most moved to surrounding towns.

With the invention of the outboard motor more and

more people stayed at the edges rather than in the middle of the basin. The outboard could get them to their nets or traps quickly and bring them back to Bayou Sorrel, Henderson or Maringouin to the comforts of electricity, television, running water, telephones, and air conditioning.

But to most of these folks and their offspring the basin still plays an important role in their lives. Many use camps deep in the swamp for hunting or fishing. Bayou Chene now has a high bank that is suitable for campsites and many former Bayou Chene residents have built nice camps near the buried village they grew up in over fifty years ago. Some of these folks from New Iberia, Franklin, and Plaquemine spend half their time on the bayou banks of the Chene.

Calvin Voisin and Gwen Carpenter both have relatives who lived in Bayou Chene. Perhaps this is what drew them back to live in the basin.

Their home is really something else—maybe not one you would see in *Better Homes and Gardens*, but to me it's a palace. It all started when the one-room cabin they were living in on Jakes Bayou was taken by the 1973 flood. It wasn't the water that did the damage, even though the flood line was over their heads. It was the mud. Such a heavy load settled in their house, the floor gave way. Not about to let that happen again, Calvin and Gwen went looking for something flood proof. By chance they found a steel barge, built in 1925 with a sturdy riveted hull. Then they purchased an old four-square house from the Millie Plantation, took it apart, hauled it over the levee, and with a crude sketch began to piece together their future home.

Gwen told me, "It took us seven months to build this house and we worked every day but Sunday. Saturday night we'd treat ourselves to a quart of beer each, flop down exhausted, and listen to the Old South Jamboree on the radio."

It's amazing what a dedicated pair can do once they set their minds to it. Despite hammered thumbs and aching muscles, they put the house together without any power tools. Sawing the heavy cypress roof timbers, Gwen said, "Calvin would start and saw until he got tired, then I would take over, then Calvin would finally finish it. People would come by and give us no encouragement at all. Some would say our house would never stay up."

Without prior building experience, Calvin and Gwen finished their new home and pushed it back to Jakes Bayou. Now they are settled, and their rusty old barge with the weatherbeaten cypress house on top blends right into the surrounding swamp. On its deck, grape vines grow up around wooden planter boxes holding shallots, lettuce, or hot peppers. The front porch is their favorite place, airy and almost mosquito-proof. Here they sleep in the summer on a bed that drops from the ceiling. The kitchen takes the porch's place as the most important room during the winter. The woodstove is used for warmth as well as for slow and delicious cooking.

Speaking of cooking, I had the best meal I've ever eaten at Calvin's and Gwen's one summer day. We had fresh tomatoes, corn, and okra from the garden. We had catfish and crabs from the hoopnets and some of their homemade hot sauce from the cupboard. Calvin fried the catfish to perfection. Gwen cooked a

crab and okra stew and boiled the corn. That was the first ear of corn I ever ate without butter. It was tender but crunchy, and the taste . . . out of this world. I guess the choupique that they use for fertilizer makes the corn so good.

You might say they are sort of an odd couple. Third cousins, Calvin was born on a houseboat in the swamp and Gwen grew up in the outskirts of Baton Rouge where she stayed to get a master's in speech at Louisiana State University. Before they got together, Calvin did some surveying while Gwen managed a whippet kennel, lectured and cared for exotic animals at a zoo in Philadelphia, and cooked on a tugboat. Together their talents of writing, poetry, fishing, gardening, welding, and photography make their life in the swamp not only peaceful, but interesting.

Another young swamper, quite different from Calvin and Gwen, is Johnny Johnson.

I met Johnny and his crawfish partner, Wilbert Hebert, late in May one year. I was heading out Bayou Pigeon to do some exploring and landscape photography at Grand Lake when I noticed a red and green bateau coming out of the woods loaded with fifteen sacks of crawfish. It was late in the season, the water was low, and hardly anybody was catching more than a sack or two, so I turned to meet them.

I idled on over, cut my engine, and introduced myself. Talking about their good catch, we drifted slowly down the bayou. "The reason for our success?" Wilbert mused. "I guess we try harder and have a good spot." I mentioned I'd like pictures of some good crawfishermen and they invited me to join them the next day.

I met them just before 6:00 the next morning at Berthelot's landing. With both boats in the water we quickly cast off. Heading out, we passed one of their cousins pulling catfish off a trot line across the Baton Rouge-Morgan City Barge Canal. The sun, today a giant orange ball, burned away the bayou mist as it peered over the levee. I yearned to stop and photograph it, but today was for crawfishing.

Not many crawfish were being caught because the water level was already very low. We stopped at the Pigeon gauge and saw it had dropped another two-tenths since yesterday. Wilbert said we might have to drag our boats part of the way.

Once in the small bayou where I had met them the day before, we had to block our motors up so they wouldn't drag bottom. Soon we had to get out and pull. Johnny told Wilbert that by the weekend their season would be over, but today it was beautiful. The soft sunlight began filtering through the canopy of feathery leaves, giving a greenish glow to the morning. We found their pirogues. As they poled through the cathedral-like path of milk chocolate waters toward their traps, I knew why these young men loved the swamp so.

Soon I watched them pull their chicken-wire (now called crawfish-wire in south Louisiana) traps from the water. Each had two to five pounds of nice size crawfish. They baited the traps with a shad-like fish, pogie, that comes from the East Coast. "Crawfish love it," Johnny says. "It stinks."

By noon, with half their traps run, Johnny and Wilbert had eight sacks. Still a few good days left.

Back at the bateaus I joined them for a typical swamper's lunch. Out of a beat-up ice chest Wilbert pulled a loaf of white bread, some sandwich spread, packaged ham, a few canned cokes, and small bags of potato chips. I can assure you they eat a lot better when they cook a gumbo or some rabbit stew at their camp.

I asked them what they would do after crawfish season. "Maybe do a little crabbing," Johnny said. Johnny works with a painting contractor sometimes during the off season, a job his wife Carolyn occasionally wishes he would stick to for more security.

Johnny or Wilbert could never last as painters. Their love for the swamp is too great. Johnny summed up his feelings best by telling me something that was close to my own dreams. "You know, when I die if I had a choice of going back and seeing the virgin cypress in the basin or going to heaven, I'd take the cypress."

LANDSCAPE

The baldcypress is a big part of the Atchafalaya Basin's landscape. Not only is it quite impressive growing up to 150 feet tall and over 6 feet wide, but also it is simply beautiful. Most people just associate the cypress with the swamp. Actually, though, this river basin swamp can be divided into four distinct landscapes: hardwood bottomland, cypress-tupelo swamp, coastal marsh, and the bay with its newly created islands. All of these plant communities work together to play an important role in the basin's productiveness.

To get a real feeling for the landscape here, it's best to drift through the seasons of the swamp.

Winter

Winter can be pleasant in the Atchafalaya if you are inclined to enjoy the cold. I do and camp frequently at this time of the year. On a two-night trip in January I woke after a bone-chilling night to find crystal clear skies at sunrise, a sure sign that the temperature had dropped to well below freezing. My canteen had ice in it, verifying the sky's indication. My breakfast of hot cocoa and scrambled eggs warmed me somewhat. Then I hiked into the woods.

First I crossed a dry slough into a cypress forest. It had no water and no underbrush, just a light carpet of leaves. I felt like I was alone in a large auditorium. The high branches of the cypress formed a patchwork roof over my head. I could hear the Carolina wren and see a pair of chickadees up ahead.

On the other side of this cypress break I came to a small bayou, unnamed on the map. I call it Classic Cut. It's one of my favorite small streams, for it has an old, half-hollow tree I like to photograph in all seasons. Classic Cut was low and had only a slight flow. I waded downstream, passing a cypress knee with a rim of ice around it. The bayou must have dropped, leaving an icy skirt almost like a ballerina's tutu around this knee. On down the cut I came to a small pond where the bayou spread out, its entire surface covered with a thin sheet of ice. A short distance across I noticed a puff of breath fog emerge from the end of a hollow log. Bending down, I saw a nutria and three pups hiding inside. Knowing they were seen, the mother and her threesome leaped out, crashed through the ice and swam away underwater.

On down the bayou I came to a larger pond, almost dry except for where the stream passed through its center. The mud around the edges had cracked up into plate-size chunks. Bits of grass were growing between the cakes of mud, some of which had hardened egret tracks on them. I also found sunbleached crawfish heads and the broken skull of a beaver.

Historical records show the beaver only in the eastern part of Louisiana. Today, though, he is increasing his range and is commonly found in this area of the spillway.

As it warmed up, clouds began to gather. Rain tonight. I guessed we'd be having typical winter weather by midnight. I unbuttoned my jacket and headed back to camp. My tent needed some improvements to ward off the rain. First I put up my emergency space blanket as a rain fly, then I tied my front and rear poles off in two directions for extra support, and finally I dug a little drainage ditch around the tent to keep standing water from building up underneath.

When my living quarters were secure I realized I was hungry. Having a roaring campfire is perhaps the best thing about sleeping out; I hurried to build one. You're never alone with a fire, its smoke twisting up through the branches, its flames dancing in the breeze, and its wood crackling to the tune of nearby wild things. It warms you. It cooks your meals. It comforts your fears.

I tossed a burger and a plump yellow squash wrapped in aluminum foil into the coals. Supper was ready in no time and, like most outdoor meals, was delicious.

The fire smoldered down to ash and coals as I glanced around the sky. Clouds being pushed by a rising wind gave a quick glimpse of a star here and there. Sleep captured me.

Awhile later I woke up. A drop of rain hit my cheek, then another. It was pitch dark, the fire was out, and I was a bit cold. The drizzle turned to rain as I crawled to my tent and into my sleeping bag.

It rained off and on all night. The wind blew and the lightning must have been near, for I could feel vibrations of the thunder. Luckily I had tied my tent down; the gust certainly would have knocked over my normal riggings. Tomorrow would be a muddy day, but soon winter would be ushered out with the red-maple flowers and the yellow-top bloom. The water would rise and the tips of the willow branches would turn red. Almost imperceptibly the elm would bear its seed and the hawks begin circling. As winter exits the mallards fly in pairs and the barred owl hoots a different song.

Spring

Now is the time the unlearned get lost. The waters seek the tops of the bayou banks and then pour over into the woods, the lakes, and the backswamps. No longer can you tell if you are on a named water course or drifting out of control through a clearing in the forest.

Even veteran swampers get turned around, but they know to follow the current, the wind, or the sun until they reach a familiar landmark and regain the right track.

I've never been turned around for more than a day, and when I was it didn't really matter. Being halfway lost just adds excitement to exploring. It would be hard to go hungry in the Atchafalaya.

The high water comes right up to the rapidly greening branches, even covering some after they have already borne their leaves.

In the backswamp I have watched the tupelos put forth a showy display of their obovate, sometimes toothed, lime green leaves. Then I've come back a week later to see an army of caterpillars eating the last few brand new leaves. The rest of the forest, already green, watches the naked tupelos struggle to put on another coat by mid-May.

By the time the full green arrives, some birds are leaving. The yellowthroat, the myrtle warbler, and the yellow-bellied sapsucker depart for the north, but the parula and the prothonotary warbler return from the south just in time to eat the caterpillars that devoured the tupelo leaves.

The bayou banks are lit in yellows from the swamp privet's tiny flower and in reds and blacks from the dewberry's fruit. Tangles of poison ivy, trumpet-creeper, smilax, ratten-vine, and pepper-vine close in the once open space in the floor of the forest.

Whether it's an illusion or scientifically accurate, I don't know, but one spring day when the conditions are just right, it seems as if every water snake in the basin comes out to sun itself on a log or a shrub sticking out of the warming waters—hundreds of snakes on one short piece of bayou.

I noticed this phenomenon a number of times, one of which in particular really stands out in my mind. I needed to get a springtime shot from my time lapse stand on Big Bayou Mallet, but my canoe was hidden in a backswamp near a rookery. I decided to call my

It was a small bateau, only ten feet long. Grey's walking in the boat was causing more danger than the harmless water snakes could ever offer.

I ordered, "Sit down, Grey, they're harmless water snakes. And really, I didn't expect this to happen."

I continued down the bayou. Snakes were everywhere. A log blocking most of the bayou got Grey on his feet again. It was full of snakes. Grey tried to climb on top of the outboard motor.

I stopped the motor and got him to sit down by convincing him he was safer in the boat than falling into the water. As the day passed I think Grey lost some of his fear of snakes, simply because we saw so many and he made it back safely. Perhaps he even convinced himself that all snakes are not evil.

All animals seem to run wild in the springtime. The mating, nest building, food gathering, and special plumes and colors make them highly visible. Towards summer when the mosquito swarms hit their peak most animals begin to slow down.

Summer

Mosquitos—you just don't find a swamp without these pesky little creatures. I'm pretty used to the blood suckers in the basin now; I guess I've been bitten so many times I'm immune. But once, at the beginning of the summer of 1975, I met a swarm I couldn't stand.

Bill McCall and I had gone out for a recreational, overnight canoe trip. The water was still very high because that was a flood year. It was a sunny day, and with our shirts off we fished and swam and explored little sloughs through the woods. When it started getting toward dark I began to realize that we had not seen a bayou bank that was not covered with water.

I got out my map and saw a pipeline up ahead about two miles that might have a bank out of the water. We paddled hard and got there just before dark. One pointed lump about ten feet in diameter stuck out of the water. Although it looked like an inverted bowl, this hill would have to do.

We managed to get the tent up before the mosquitos came, but the little buzzing bombers hit us hard during supper. The meal was junked and we leaped into the tent along with fifty mosquitos, cutting another thousand off at the pass when I closed the zipper.

Bill was concerned about those inside.

I said, "Lie down, I'll show you an old Boy Scout trick." Bill lay on his side of the hill, which slanted at 35 degrees to the south, and I did the same on my side, which slanted to the north. "Now," I said. "Take the flashlight and point it at the ceiling. All the mosquitos should go up the apex of the tent."

They did, and I rubbed each one into the cloth of the tent.

With that task out of the way, we noticed the sound. Buzzzzzzzzing.

Bill estimated a million of them out there. Through the mosquito net door, a solid swarm of the tiny devils with their razor-sharp sucking tubes just waited for the chance to sink into our tender skin. I caught a glimpse of a big yellow moon, but it quickly was hidden, by the masses. "Bill," I said in frustration, "Tonight there's a full moon and they are blocking it from my view. I don't believe it." I tried to sleep.

friend who had been wanting to go into the swamp with me, but we just hadn't gotten around to it yet. He had access to a small bateau with a motor.

I called and Grey said he could go, but he was apprehensive about snakes. I told him I had been in a similar area three days ago and had not seen a single one. "I don't think they are out yet," I assured him.

When he reiterated his fear of these reptiles, I returned my truthful and standard answer: "If we do see any, nine out of ten will be harmless water snakes. I've seen thousands in my time, and if you are careful you won't have any problems. They have no reason to attack you. Keep your distance and you're safe." He was somewhat assured and we left.

Well, it turned out to be one of those extra warm spring days. As we put the boat in the water I knew I was wrong—we would see a snake. But I kept quiet about my new knowledge.

Shortly, it happened—a snake explosion. As I was running the boat slowly down a small bayou every available branch, limb, log, and stump had one, two, even four snakes on it.

Grey just about flipped out. He yelled, "Stay in the middle! . . . Don't go near the sides! . . . I thought you said there would be no snakes!" He stood up, went to the front of the boat, then came back by me in a panic.

An hour later, I had to urinate; Bill begged me to stay in the tent, but I had to go. I put on socks, shoes, jeans, long sleeved shirt and a hat and wrapped a towel around my neck. I climbed through the zipper quickly, wishing I had some gloves too.

Mosquitos came from everywhere. The jeans did no good. They bit right through. Needless to say I couldn't concentrate on my mission, so after I jumped back into the tent Bill and I went through the Boy Scout trick again and faked sleep for the rest of the night.

Never have I seen them that bad again. It must have been the high water, the moon—or who knows?

As summer moves along, the vibrant greens of spring turn to just a ho-hum green. The water drops fast. The heat slows everything down, even the mosquitos.

The only action comes from violent but short-lived thunderstorms. A summer night in a tupelo-gum swamp can be frightening when the purple skies are cracked open with bolts of lightning silhouetting the weird forms of the gum trees. I am sure this is when and where every witch's tale was brewed.

Annual spring flowers have left behind only the occasional lavender blanket of the water hyacinths. Some lakes are covered from end to end, resembling the poppy field that put Dorothy and her friends to sleep in the Wizard of Oz. This menace, now almost three feet high in places, is impassable in most crafts. Only a determined Cajun with a pointed skiff weighed down with 400 pounds of crawfish and his Mercury 50 can burst through this floating mass of plantlife.

The hyacinth, introduced to America at the International Cotton Exposition in New Orleans in 1884, is good in one respect, for it blocks off many backswamp areas from all but the hardiest of men. This blockade makes many miniature wildlife refuges where plants and animals alike can rest from man's intrusions.

The Japanese who brought the hyacinth here found it in South America and thought it would make a nice souvenir to give out at the Exposition. It was liked, all right, and taken home and put in backyard ponds all over the state. Today, after spreading successfully, water hyacinths cover much of Louisiana waters.

It's a hardy flower and quite prolific. A single plant can produce up to 60,000 offspring in just one summer. I was told that the hyacinth was once used to make fiber board. It was ground up, pressed together and used in house construction. When a rain came to the construction site, the carpenters watched the water hyacinths sprout out of the wall. I don't know if I really believe that one or not, but I can vouch for the hyacinth's staying powers.

Soon the purple flowers wilt, the days grow shorter, and a new season is here.

Fall

Autumn in the basin is my favorite time of the year. September brings the first sign of its approach: the ibis leave the coast to fish for mussel shells exposed upon the bayou banks and lake beds. Most animals become more active and concentrated as water levels continue to go down. Interconnected lakes become individual ponds, shallow and full of easy prey for the wading birds, raccoons, mink, and otters.

Now is also the time for hurricanes on the coast and other frontal systems that push out the heat and haze and make way for clear, clean, blue skies dressed with slight wisps of clouds that produce September and October sunsets—the most beautiful in the basin. And the moonrise, the harvest moon! Fall is one of the few times of the year you can be assured that neither clouds nor storms will block its awesome rising. Fall is also a perfect time for camp-outs, especially for those who do not want to experience the cold of the winter, the high waters of spring, and the insects of the summer.

Under a gorgeous harvest moon I camped in the Grand River Flats with some friends. Most had been canoeing and camping before, but all were relatively inexperienced. It was a picture perfect Saturday morning when we left the levee in seven canoes and one strange contraption. Its builder claimed it was a kayak; I thought it was a pregnant pirogue, but it worked almost as well as a canoe.

We paddled against the current. A few went slowly at first, but soon all had control of their crafts. Just as everyone began to relax, we turned off Grand River and went into a small slough coming out of Upper Flat Lake. It wasn't much more than a trickle, six inches deep and two feet wide. The slough was too shallow for paddles and too muddy for pulling. The comments flew among my friends as canoes clanked into each other. "Looks like this would be more enjoyable coming down" . . . "I'm tired" . . . "How far does this go?" . . . and, "I thought canoeing was supposed to be fun."

I told them to take it easy, this thing only went about a quarter of a mile and tomorrow it would be a lot more fun with the current, so just think about the easy trip home.

Soon we were in the big lake and everyone was laughing again, looking at the ancient cypress stumps jutting out of the still waters of the flats. At the opposite end of the lake we found a cypress-studded island half covered by tall, green grass and half bare with hard sand and mussel shells. My well-used two-man green tent, speckled with dark red spots of mosquitos that had so valiantly tried to do battle with my flashlight, was joined by a brilliant array and styling of blue and orange mountain tents to make our little island quite appealing.

While one orange structure was being erected in the grass, a young coon ran from his resting place into a hollow log, out the other end, then swam a short distance and climbed a dead cypress tree. There the little fellow with the bandit face watched us finish making camp.

Besides the raccoon we noticed much wildlife from our island campsite. Across the lake we saw hundreds of birds. Closer inspection with binoculars revealed great egrets, snowy egrets, little blue herons, and Louisiana herons feeding on the crawfish and minnows confined to small ponds between the willow ridges and cypress islands. A couple of mallards swam in one of the larger ponds while an anhinga dried her wings on top of a short stump. A spotted sandpiper bobbed its head at the water's edge.

The tips of the willows were showing the first signs of yellow and a few stumps were full of tangles of trumpet creeper with its orange flowers in full bloom. The baldcypress still had its full coat of green leaves and would need a good wet cold snap to make them turn.

Our crew split up after lunch. Some fished, some went to watch the birds, and some went exploring. By early evening the lake was aglow. Our troops began returning. Some set up tripods and waited for what we expected to be a great sunset. Others were being entertained by a preying mantis crawling in someone's hair. The fishermen returned with a bass and a blue gill and decided to save them for breakfast. The explorers, traveling through the many inter-connected lakes and bayous, saw nutria, wood ducks and an alligator. The bird watchers got a closer look at the herons and a family of coons that came up to one of the ponds at sunset.

The chill of night soon began to set in, and thoughts turned to a roaring campfire. Just as the last twilight flickered out, gasps rose from the campfire crew. The harvest moon was rising over the lake. I photographed our group, the campfire, and the moon. When the newness of the moon wore off, we became acutely aware of hunger pangs. We had all brought our own menus. Burgers, steaks, and stews were carefully put into the coals. After dinner I told the story of the famous "swamp wolf." Then everybody contributed favorite ghost stories as the moon rose higher and brightened the slick waters of the lake with its silver glow. At last the talk slowed down as the day's sun, exercise and good food brought sleep to all our eyes.

The morning was thick with fog. Visibility was less than ten feet. We could not see the tops of the trees above us. Three canoes took off for some fishing. I followed to photograph them disappearing and reappearing in the mist. They fished hard, but only the Old Town Canoe carrying Al McDuff and the "Old Beachcomber," Bob Scearce, returned successfully with a stringer of sac-a-lait.

The sun began to burn off the fog as I prepared the breakfast fire. Most everybody was around the fishermen, trying to get in on the panfried fish. In a big black iron skillet, I cooked my camping breakfast special: potatoes, tomatoes, eggs, cheese, bacon and onions all mixed and fried together. Nobody bothered my breakfast; it's good, though.

We broke camp at lunch, but no one hurried home. By mid-afternoon the canoes were grouped and aiming happily down the shallow slough. At Grand River we stopped for a swim. There was a nice sandbar exposed. Someone found that the sand was kind of gooey at the water's edge, and a mud fight developed. Later, when we all took another swim to clean off, the surface was warm, but below a deep current, probably from the depths of the Atchafalaya River, ran icy cold and very refreshing.

Back at the landing the architects, lawyers, nurses, and the others prepared to re-enter civilization—as I did for the evening. But the next day I unlashed my canoe and hooked up my bateau to take another fall trip into another Flat Lake just above Morgan City.

It's funny how there are so many Flat Lakes, Grand Rivers, Old Rivers, Black Lakes and Bayou Blacks throughout the country. But think about this: what if you were the one to discover the Grand Canyon, or Yellowstone, or the Atchafalaya Basin? Could you come up with different and unique names for millions of birds, trees, mountains, canyons, lakes, and rivers?

Monday morning I knew exactly where I was going—to a beautiful baldcypress break on the east side of Flat Lake. Here I had been planning a perfect Louisiana swamp sunset. I put in at Little Bayou Sorrel and crossed the Port Allen-Morgan City barge route while the fog was almost as thick as yesterday's.

The area between Little Bayou Sorrel and Flat Lake is criss-crossed by many small, intermingling bayous: Bear Bayou, Bayou Cane, Bayou Cocodrie, Bayou Chevreuil, and Bayou Grosbeak. All day I drifted and poled and waded these waterways, having fun and killing time till sunset. I saw a mink on Bayou Chevreuil and a bass fisherman on Bayou Cocodrie, but otherwise it was just me and the birds.

An hour before sunset I went to my chosen place and set up my tripod among the cypress knees. The water here was clear and blackish, about one foot deep. Getting wet all the time is hard on my tripods, but that's just part of my job. In my viewfinder I had five nice baldcypress trees, each hung with moss. I also had a few nice knees sticking out of the glassy water. When the sun finally hit the tree line a mile across the lake the sky, the clouds, and the water picked up its brilliant colors. And just as I hit the shutter a bass jumped to make a nice splash and add life to the photograph.

I can feel that vibrant scene to my bones. Never will I forget it, nor will I forget the Atchafalaya Basin.

WILDLIFE

Silky feathers grown for courtship and nesting decorate this male Great Egret as he stands guard over recently hatched youngsters.

Resting on one leg, a yellow-crowned night heron yawns while napping upon a cypress branch. Only moments before, he had been at the bayou bank quietly waiting for a meal to swim by. In rapid succession he had nabbed five or six crawfish with a lightning-fast strike and swallowed them whole—tail first, of course. Besides the night heron, raccoons, opossums, otters, egrets, ibis, owls, hawks, bass, and man seek this delicious crustacean. During a good year like 1978, the basin will produce more than 1.5 billion crawfish to feed the multitudes of other animals.

Overbank-flooding each spring perpetuates the Atchafalaya's crawfish crop. These, along with numerous other aquatic creatures, start the basic food chains for over 300 species of birds, 46 species of mammals, 53 species of reptiles, 28 species of amphibians, 90 species of fish, and thousands of kinds of insects, worms, mollusks, crustaceans and other lower forms. Is the Atchafalaya Basin a wildlife paradise? Thanks to the crawfish, the answer is a most definite, "yes."

With a yearly population reaching more than one billion individuals, the crawfish (left) is one of the most important species of wildlife in the Atchafalaya. These multitudes form the basis of a food chain that feeds many animals such as the Yellow-crowned Night Heron (above).

The massive loads of silt that pour into the Atchafalaya Bay are building a new wildlife habitat. The Least Tern was one of the first species to take advantage of these islands. Once the terns have selected a nest site the male stages a complex ceremony of presenting a minnow to his mate (top and middle left). This leads to copulation (middle right), egg laying (lower left), and hatching of the young terns (lower right).

Right
Partially camouflaged by leaves and moss, the Barred Owl tries to stay out of sight during the day. At night his seven-hoot tune is one of the magical sounds of the swamp.

Like a statue, a Snowy Egret pauses during feeding on a tidal mud flat in the lower Atchafalaya (below). Later, White and Glossy Ibis who have left the same feeding grounds fly silhouetted against the setting sun (left).

Below
On the forest floor a wolf spider waits
patiently for a chance to leap upon
unsuspecting prey.

Right
Not quite ready to fly but agile enough to
hop down from their nest hole, two young
Barred Owls take their first look at Sawyer's Cove, their future hunting grounds.

One of the few dry spots the Atchafalaya has during the spring high water is in the trees. Raccoons (left) sleep among the branches, and Red-shouldered Hawks (bottom) make their nest here. The Green Tree Frog (below) climbs up small trees at night to call for a mate.

Fear seems to shine from the face of a young flying squirrel (below) and a fledgling Louisiana Heron (far right) as they get the evil eye from an outstretched broad-banded water snake. But the fear is unjustified for this snake's diet consists mainly of fish and other small aquatic creatures.

Left
Christmas in October as the red of a
cardinal flower contrasts beautifully with
the surrounding green vegetation. A
passing cloudless sulphur butterfly is the
ornament.

Above
The White-tail Deer is a prolific breeder
when the conditions are right, thus it can
bounce back to a healthy population within
a few years of a major flood.

Right
Buttonbush is the major understory plant in
the Atchafalaya and many birds like the
Least Bittern use it as a nesting site. These
four young birds point their beaks into the
air, an act that will camouflage them once
they get their adult feathers.

Right
Lady bugs mating on a
hydrocotyle leaf.

Left
On certain days in the early
spring, every log and every
branch has a snake on it.
Rarely do they fall into
a passing boat.

Below
With sensuous curves and
pure white feathers, the
Great Egret is the most
beautiful bird of the
swamps.

Through an almost solid mat of alligator
weed, two young nutria pop up to inspect
the photographer.

The Swamp Canary, better known as the Prothonotary Warbler, sings its sweet, sweet song from a perch near its nest (left). A Tiger Swallowtail butterfly excretes a substance from its tail (below).

Crawling back to Upper Grand River, a Red-eared Turtle has just finished laying her eggs.

Above
Little things are a big part of the Atchafalaya Basin's ecosystem. Even the water bugs skating over a fog-covered lake are important to the swamp's chain of life.

Right
Lands accreting in Atchafalaya Bay make excellent winter habitat for many species of water fowl. Here, a group of teal rests in the early morning sun.

Right
Although it is not native to the Atchafalaya or even to Louisiana, the fire ant has adapted amazingly well to swamp life. In high water they simply form a floating ball of ants, rolling over and over to take turns being under water.

A large-mouth bass is in hot pursuit of a sailfin molly (above).

Looking like a floating log, an alligator rests among aquatic plants in an egret rookery where the author spent many hours.

Perched in the fork of an oak tree, the
opossum, North America's most primitive
mammal, peers at the photographer in a
nearby tree.

Left
Tangles of lacy Baldcypress leaves hide this Yellow-crowned Night Heron's nest from view. This tree had six nests in it.

SWAMPERS

Swamper supreme, Alciede Verrett is in his late seventies. He is still pulling up hoop nets and is more active than most men in their forties.

Before the Civil War, several sugar cane plantations produced a substantial crop in the Atchafalaya Basin. Then at the turn of the century a highly profitable red cypress industry had its short heyday there. Today the petroleum industry is pumping millions of dollars worth of irreplaceable oil and gas from the basin. The one industry that hasn't depleted itself (and is in no danger so long as we leave the swamp wet and wild) is fishing. From the time of the Chitimacha Indians to modern man, people have been fishing for a living in the Atchafalaya Swamp.

Most of the few old swampers who dwell in the basin year-around fish for a living. They drag hoop-nets up from the deep Atchafalaya River, or dip shad from its banks, or bait trot lines with river shrimp. Others live in small towns along the levee, but pole through the cathedral-like canopy of trees to make their living catching crawfish.

Still others come with rods and reels to cast a spinner bait toward a shore-bound log, hoping to catch a bass. And a few come without any fishing gear, escaping some noisy and polluted urban area to drift aimlessly across a mirrored lake with their thoughts focused on the reflections of the black water.

For each of these people, the Atchafalaya successfully satisfies a different need.

Tending the arbor where grape vines, hot peppers, and flowers grow on the front of their house barge, Calvin Voisin and Gwen Carpenter are some of the few young people who live in the swamp full-time (right).

Calvin and Alciede work together on many fishing projects, this day to no avail for the crappie they caught in their hoop net is classified a sport fish and has to be returned to the bayou (below).

The morning sun shrouded by bayou mist gives a dreamlike glow to Calvin and Gwen's house barge (left). Mornings are slow in the fall, and the swinging bed on their front porch is a good place for sipping tea. Emily Lou, their tailless dog, begs for some attention (below).

Surrounding towns are also awakening. The levee at Henderson supports the houses and camps of many a Cajun fisherman.

Left
Calvin pulls a hoop net full of wiggling "fiddlers", his word for young blue or channel catfish, from the Atchafalaya River.

Calvin and Gwen come as close to living off the land as anybody these days. The chickens Gwen feeds (above left) provide their eggs, while Calvin supplies their fish with a blue catfish caught on one of his trot lines (above right).

The surplus fish are taken to Bayou Sorrel fish buyers in Alciede's wooden bateau.

Left
In his pirogue loaded with a hundred pounds of catfish, Alciede smiles while he talks about a sixty-six pounder he caught on a snag line years ago.

Below
Claude Metrejean (top) one of the many crawfish and fish buyers that surround the Atchafalaya Basin sometimes processes thousands of pounds of catfish a day (bottom).

Above
Lubin Jewel, an excellent cook as are most Cajun men, checks the tenderness of some roasting wood ducks at his deer camp near Maringouin.

Right
Calvin frys catfish, the best ever, amid the clutter of iron pots and herbs that hang above their propane stove.

Below
Friendly folks. The swampers always have time to share a cup of coffee with a visitor.

Food plays an important role in the
Atchafalaya. Good food and good cooks
come from the swamp.

Bitten over three hundred times by snakes while collecting them for scientific research, Kelly Falcon tries again for a Diamond-backed water snake.

When mattresses were stuffed with Spanish Moss, the swamp was alive with moss collectors. Today only a few ply this trade, and they sell their bales to minnow hatcheries.

When fall comes to the swamp, game is abundant and the woods crowded with hunters. Tents and campboats become seasonal homes for these woodsmen.

Some prefer to quietly paddle through the cypress stumps of the Grand River Flats to jig for sac-a-lait or cast for bass.

Johnny Johnson (left) and his crawfish partner Wilbert Hebert (right) paddle their pirogues back to their bateau after checking one side of their trap line.

Crawfishing is a major recreational sport. Here a family from Pride, Louisiana, spends a day catching crawfish with set nets.

There is no beginning and no end to the ways Louisianians find to spend time in the Atchafalaya. Some fish with cane poles (top left), some take guided canoe trips (lower left) and some find those lonesome and beautiful but not quite comfortable campsites for a night of slapping mosquitoes (right).

In the silent moments before dark, a bass fisherman heads home after a day of casting for lunkerheads in Lake Pelba.

There is nothing warmer than friends around a campfire. With a hearty stew under their belts this crew whiles away the evening under the harvest moon after a hard day of paddling through the swampland.

Sometimes the swamp will surprise you. Floating marsh with the consistency of molasses can make going tough. Marty Stouffer, with a rope around his waist, tries to pull his boat free (top). And just as hard to navigate are the endless patches of Water Hyacinth. Here with three paddles in action, little headway is made (above).

Who can say the swamp does not have the
magic of the mountains? There are many
moments in the evening sun's glow that
just can't be described.

Afternoon reflections present the ultimate in stillness for a pair of canoeists to enjoy.

LANDSCAPE

An October sunset at Flat Lake. More beauty exists nowhere.

Y̶ou won't find a scenic turnout in the Atchafalaya Basin unless you are inclined to hoist yourself up into a hundred-foot baldcypress tree or fly over in a helicopter. Neither method resembles sightseeing in the mountains, deserts or canyonlands of the West, where it is possible from the air-conditioned comfort of your family station wagon to exclaim roaring appreciation of the endless panorama just beyond the sign that says, "Scenic Picture Spot #6."

What you will find, though, is a serene and breathtaking landscape—harder to see, but worthwhile if you take the time and trouble to venture out by canoe or pirogue and gaze at the orange of evening framed by a forest of moss-draped trees. The tall trees standing like sentries make little reflection on the glassine water, to be broken only by a jumping fish. This quiet beauty certainly rivals the glorious western panoramas.

Now take a closer look. The swamp is alive with little things. At the buttressed and fluted

base of three baldcypress trees the scaly bark almost falls off. On up the tapering trunk, branches reach straight out bearing feather-like leaves. Sometimes the cypress knees that circle the tree just poke out of the swamp floor like a fairy ring of mushrooms; at other times they stand tall and close together like silhouettes against a big city skyline.

To get the most out of a swamp, you must view it like a movie. Savor each scene and roll around the bayou bend to enjoy the next.

In the soggy and generally wet soil of the middle basin, Baldcypress trees use their fluted and buttressed bases for support (right). In the northern Atchatalaya where the ground is higher, hardwoods grow and ridges are decorated with ferns.

72

Below
The stumps are the only reminders of the giant Baldcypress trees cut for lumber in the 1920's. Some have filled
with dirt and become planter boxes for other plants.

Sawyer's Cove on a windless day gives a reflection so perfect it is hard to tell which way is up.

Top Right
A gnarled old Baldcypress tree, probably more than four hundred years old. It is twenty feet around its trunk but only thirty-five feet tall. Lightning probably struck it hundreds of years ago and stunted its height.

Right
Some of the little things offer just as much beauty as an ancient tree. A fragrant water lily stars among the surrounding pads.

Classic Bayou seen in March, April, and August. The water level in this spot has varied as much as twelve feet. The changing water level is very important to the crawfish and other aquatic creatures of the Atchafalaya.

Left
Words can never describe a sunset, especially one viewed in nature. Grand River Flats in November.

78

Spring has sprung, and the water begins to rise. The grasses it will soon cover will offer food and protection to millions of young crawfish and other aquatic creatures.

Right, Above
Foresters and scientists have been discussing the function of cypress knees for years. No proven explanation exists, but theories run wild. Some suggest they are for extra support in the mushy swamp soil.

Right
The scaly grey bark of a Baldcypress trunk mingles with the recent fallen, feather-like leaves. In the fall the swamp is usually dry, giving time for vegetation to accumulate for the next spring.

The Water Hyacinth covers over 200,000 acres of lakes, bayous, and canals in the Atchafalaya Basin. It is sometimes known as the devil in disguise, for its beautiful flower contrasts with its nemesis of depleting the oxygen supply in the swampland waters.

Mayweed or Daisy Fleabane is a common spring wild flower in the higher areas of the basin (above) while spider-lily is much more adapted to the wetter and lower areas (below).

Left
A Black Willow cathedral lines the way into the Grand River Flats. These trees are the first to grow on newly accreted land.

High above the setting sun a great egret cups his wings to land for the night in the sturdy branches of a Baldcypress tree.

Left
Indications of the water level exist in many fashions. An icy tutu formed around a cypress knee (left above) signals a two-inch drop the night before, while water marks (left below) on a Baldcypress forest show high water at least five feet above its present level.

Right
Water Tupelo, another tree of the central basin,
sometimes grows in pure stands as seen here or it
sometimes mixes with the Baldcypress.

To the crawfish, *Senecio glabellus*, commonly known as
yellow-top, must look like a towering cypress tree looks to
us (right). This prolific spring flower covers the bayou
banks before any of the trees bear their leaves.

A few weeks earlier these campers would have had to look elsewhere for a campsite, for this cypress island was underwater for most of the spring and summer.

Left
Cocklebur, a real nuisance to hikers.

Below
A whole city of cypress knees decorate the edge of Flat Lake.

Two notches cut in a cypress trunk. The loggers of the 1920's cut these to stand in while the giant tree was sawed down.

Lined with stately Baldcypress trees dressed in their fall colors, Bayou Pigeon is one of the major waterways in the Atchafalaya.

A lake in the egret rookery goes completely dry and is covered with flowers in the fall.

Above
Shafts of sun brighten up the morning mist at the edge of Bear Bayou.

Left
Poison Ivy winding up a Sycamore tree.

At daybreak ancient cypress stumps rest in the still waters of an unnamed lake (below). The waters will leave by summer (right) and come again by late winter (bottom).

Right
Note the difference in these tall, thin individual cypress knees as compared to the tangles of connected knees on page 90. They are different where ever you may go.

The epitome of a swamp scene: vegetation floating in fog shrouded waters among moss-draped cypress trees.

A time exposure reveals three separate crashes of lightning as a summer thunderstorm prepares to pepper Bayou Sorrel.

Another unnamed lake displays fantastic colors in the soft light of the afternoon.

The buttressed base of a giant Baldcypress highlights one of many lakes in the Grand River Flats.

PROBLEMS

What took nature hundreds of years to build, man can destroy at will.
One bite of the giant dredge can . . . .

In wildness is the preservation of the world.
Henry David Thoreau

The jaws of a dredge's giant shovel chomping through the swamplands have done much to ruin that "wildness" Thoreau talks about. With man directing, the dredge, the bulldozer, and the chainsaw have leveled 22,000,000 acres of hardwood bottomland in the Mississippi Delta. They have done this in the last fifty years, and they are still chomping it up at a rate of 300,000 acres per year.

Right now the delta has only 3 million acres left, and the Atchafalaya Basin is a large portion of that. Clearing of the forest is the worst thing that could happen to the Atchafalaya Basin.

Silt is another problem—some say it's our greatest. And they are right, in a sense, for as the silt piles up the land becomes higher and easier to be cleared and transferred to some other use, such as agriculture or industry.

Silt or sediment has accumulated along our creeks, streams, bayous, and rivers for all the years that water has been flowing. About 150 years ago man began improving (he thought) our waterways. He straightened and channeled them. He snagged the logs and dug up the riffles. He built locks, dams, and levees. The water flowed straighter, faster, and did not overflow its banks. The silt, unable to spread out over Missouri, Arkansas, Ohio, and Tennessee, stayed in the fast current until it reached the Atchafalaya Basin. There the water could disperse and drop its massive load, about 135 million tons of silt per year.

All this silt is raising the level of the land in the basin. Some say it is ruining the wildlife. But after three flood years in a row, 1973-1975, despite an unprecedented silt drop, we had a record crawfish harvest of 42 million pounds in 1978.

Besides the silt, the basin has a lot of other secondary problems. Canals disrupt its natural water flow, hyacinths clog its lakes, outlaws shock its fish, and waste dumps encircle it. But none of these nuisances can compete with the main problem, land use. If you clear the basin and convert it to agriculture and industry the system dies. The sole and simple solution to saving the basin is to ensure that the forest will never be cleared. Only by this means can the Atchafalaya continue to be an asset to us all for years to come.

ACKNOWLEDGEMENTS

Since 1973 when I first ventured into the Atchafalaya Basin's interior, I have met many fine people, all of whom have been a great help in putting together this book. They, along with many old friends, gave me much of their time, advice, and moral support while I was at work on this project.

First, I would like to thank my publisher, Norman C. Ferachi, and his staff for making this book possible. Then Kahne Strickland, my office manager, for painstakingly typing and retyping my manuscript and giving helpful hints along its way. A great deal of thanks goes also to Calvin Voisin and Gwen Carpenter who were my neighbors during the writing of this book.

Hugh Batemen, Larry de la Bretonne, Dugan Sabins, and Robert Hamilton gave their expert advice on biological facts and form. And Wayne Bettoney, Chet Boze, Charles Fryling, Johnny and Carolyn Johnson, Wilbert Hebert, Robert Helm, Oliver Houck, Al McDuff, Ladimore Smith, and Alciede Verrett helped in various ways over the last few years.

I would like to thank *National Geographic Magazine* for letting me use some of the photographs I took while on assignment for them.

Many more friends and associates have helped in making this book possible and I would like to thank them all.

"For Mom and Dad and all others who appreciate the real beauty of nature. It is here we have to live, so let's enjoy it and work together to take care of our habitat, earth."

PHOTO INFORMATION

Custom prints of all photographs used in this book are available for purchase. A limited quantity are printed in sizes 16 × 20 and 11 × 14. For information please contact:

Cactus Clyde Productions
P.O. Box 14876
Baton Rouge, Louisiana 70898

Specifics on Photographs

All photographs were taken with Nikon F, F2, F2A, or FE 35mm cameras. The name of each photograph along with lens, film, and exposure (when available) is listed below.

Simple Flight. 200mm f/4 Nikkor, f/11 @ 1/60. K64.

Cover   **Cypress Point.** 500 mm f/8 Reflex-Nikkor. f/8 @ 1/30. K64. Tripod.

II   **Still Waters.** 35mm f/3.5 PC Nikkor. f/16 @ 1/60. K64. Tripod.

III-IV   **Young Egrets.** 105mm f/2.5 Nikkor. f/8 @ 1/90. K64. Strobe.

V-VI   **Sunset Flight.** 200mm f/4 Nikkor. f/4 @ 1/500. K64.

VIII   **Preening.** 500mm f/8 Reflex-Nikkor. f/8 @ 1/30. K64. Tripod.

25-26   **Guardian of the Nest.** 500 mm f/8 Reflex-Nikkor. f/8 @ 1/30. K64. Tripod.

   Yawning. 300mm f/4.5 Nikkor. f/5.6 @ 1/250. ED 200. Tripod.

Crawfish in Clover. 105mm f/4 Novoflex, f/22 @ 1/90. K64. Bellows and strobe.

27-28   **Lease Tern with Minnow.** 500 mm f/8 Reflex-Nikkor. f/8 @ 1/250. K64. Tripod.

   Least Tern Presents Minnow. 500 mm f/8 Reflex-Nikkor. f/8 @ 1/250. K64. Tripod.

   Mating. 500 mm f/8 Reflex-Nikkor. f/8 @ 1/250. K64. Tripod.

   Incubation. 500mm f/8 Reflex-Nikkor. f/8 @ 1/250. K64. Tripod.

   Birth. 105mm f/2.5 Nikkor. f/11 @ 1/125. KR.

   Barred Owl. 1000mm f/11 Reflex-Nikkor. f/11 @ 1/125. K64. Tripod.

29-30   **Heading for the Rookery.** 200 mm f/4 Nikkor. f/8 @ 1/250. K64.

   Snowy Egret. 500mm f/8 Reflex-Nikkor. f/8 @ 1/60. ED 200. Tripod.

31-32   **Wolf Spider.** 105 mm f/4 Novoflex. f/22 @ 1/90. K64. Bellows and strobe.

   Young Owls. 200mm f/4 Nikkor. f/8 @ 1/125. K64.

33-34   **Coon.** 200mm f/4 Nikkor. f/8 @ 1/250. K64.

   Green Tree Frog. 105 mm f/4 Novoflex. f/22 @ 1/90. K64. Bellows and strobe at night.

   Red-shouldered Hawk. 105mm f/2.5 Nikkor. f/5.6 @ 1/250. K64. Monopod.

35-36   **Snake Eyes.** 55mm f/3.5 Micro-Nikkor. f/11 @ 1/125. K64.

   Peeking. 200 mm f/4 Nikkor. f/4 @ 1/125. K64.

   Young Louisiana Heron. 200mm f/4 Nikkor. f/5.6 @ 1/250. ED 200.

37-38   **Sippin' Nectar.** 55mm f/3.5 Micro-Nikkor. f/16 @ 1/60. K64. Tripod.

   White-tail Doe. 200mm f/4 Nikkor. f/11 @ 1/125. K64. Tripod.

   Least Bitterns. 55mm f/3.5 Micro-Nikkor. f/11 @ 1/125. ED 200.

39-40   **Broad-banded Water Snake.** 105mm f/2.5 Nikkor. f/16 @ 1/8. K64. Tripod.

   Great Egret. 1000mm f/11 Nikkor-Reflex. f/11 @ 1/60. K64. Tripod.

   Ladybugs. 105mm f/4 Novoflex. f/22 @ 1/90. K64. Bellows and strobe.

41-42.   **Nutria.** 1000mm f/11 Nikkor-Reflex. f/11 @ 1/125. K64. Tripod.

   Prothonotary Warbler. 1000mm f/11 Nikkor-Reflex. f/11 @ 1/125. K64. Tripod.

   Tiger Swallowtail. 200mm f/4 Nikkor. f/5.6 @ 1/125. K64.

   Red-eared Turtle. 55mm f/3.5 Micro-Nikkor. f/11 @ 1/125. K64.

43-44   **Water Bugs.** 24mm f/2.8 Nikkor. f/5.6 @ 1/60. K64.

   Green-wing Teal. 1000mm f/11 Nikkor-Reflex. f/11 @ 1/60. K64. Tripod.

   Fire Ants. 55mm f/3.5 Micro-Nikkor. f/11 @ 1/60. K64.

45-46   **Largemouth Bass.** 105mm f/2.5 Nikkor. f/16 @ 1/90. ED 200. Tripod. Four strobes in aquarium.

   Alligator. 300mm f/4.5 Nikkor. f/8 @ 1/125. ED 200.

   Opossum. 200mm f/4 Nikkor. f/8 @ 1/250. ED 200.

47-48   **Yellow-crowned Night Heron.** 500mm f/8 Nikkor/Reflex. f/8 @ 1/60. K64. Tripod.

   Insect. 105mm f/4 Novoflex. f/22 @ 1/90. K64. Bellows and strobe.

49-50   **Alciede Verrett.** 105mm f/2.5 Nikkor. f/5.6 @ 1/30. ED 200.

House Barge. 55mm f/3.5 Micro-Nikkor. f/8 @ 1/60. K64.

Hoopnets. 35mm f/3.5 PC Nikkor. f/8 @ 1/125. K64.

51-52   **House Barge at Dawn.** 55mm f/3.5 Micro-Nikkor. f/8 @ 1/125. K64.

Swinging Bed. 55mm f/3.5 Micro-Nikkor. f/8 @ 1/15. K64. Tripod.

Henderson, La. 24mm f/2.8 Nikkor. f/4 @ 1/2000. ED 200. From airplane.

53-54   **Calvin and Hoopnets.** 24mm f/2.8 Nikkor. f/8 @ 1/125. ED 200.

Gwen and Chickens. 24mm f/2.8 Nikkor. f/11 @ 1/125. ED 200.

Calvin and Trout Line. 24mm f/2.8 Nikkor. f/11 @ 1/125. K64.

Alciede's Bateau. 135mm f/2.8 Nikkor. f/4 @ 1/500. K64.

55-56   **Alciede in Pirogue.** 55mm f/3.5 Micro-Nikkor. f/11 @ 1/125. K64.

Claude Metrejean. 35mm f/3.5 PC Nikkor. f/3.5 @ 1/30. K64.

Catfish Cleaners. 24mm f/2.8 Nikkor. f/8 @ 1/90. K64. Strobe.

57-58   **Cooking Ducks and Biscuits.** 24mm f/2.8 Nikkor. f/11 @ 1/90. K64. Strobe.

Frying Catfish. 55mm f/3.5 Micro-Nikkor. f/8 @ 1/90. K64. Strobe.

Oysters and Crawfish. 24mm f/2.8 Nikkor. f/5.6 @ 1/90. K64. Strobe.

Visiting. 24mm f/2.8 Nikkor. f/8 @ 1/30. K64. Self-timed.

59-60   **Kelly Falcon.** 55mm f/3.5 Micro-Nikkor. f/5.6 @ 1/250. K64.

Moss Men. 24mm f/2.8 Nikkor. f/8 @ 1/250. K64.

Campboat. 105mm f/2.5 Nikkor. f/8 @ 1/125. K64.

Foggy Fishing in Upper Flats. 500mm f/8 Nikkor-Reflex f/8 @ 1/60. Tripod.

61-62   **Johnny Johnson.** 24mm f/2.8 Nikkor. f/11 @ 1/500. ED 200

Wilbert Hebert and Johnny Johnson. 24mm f/2.8 Nikkor. f/8 @ 1/125. K64.

Crawfishing Family. 105mm f/2.5 Nikkor. f/8 @ 1/125. K64.

63-64   **Cane Pole Fishing.** 105mm f/2.5 Nikkor. f/8 @ 1/125. K64.

Canoeing. 105mm f/2.5 Nikkor. f/11 @ 1/125. K64.

Campsite. 55mm f/3.5 Micro-Nikkor. f/8 @ 1/30. K64.

65-66   **Heading Home.** 55mm f/3.5 Micro-Nikkor. f/5.6 @ 1/500. K64. From top of oil derrick.

67-68   **Campfire.** 55mm f/3.5 Micro-Nikkor. f/3.5 @ one minute. ED 200. Tripod.

Marty Stouffer. 24mm f/2.8 Nikkor. f/8 @ 1/250. K64.

Three Canoeists. 105mm f/2.5 Nikkor. f/5.6 @ 1/250. Tripod.

69-70   **Sunset Tents.** 500mm f/8 Nikkor-Reflex. f/8 @ 1/8. K64. Tripod.

Canoeist. 200mm f/4 Nikkor. f/4 @ 1/250. K64.

71-72   **Flat Lake Sunset.** 35mm f/3.5 PC Nikkor. f/11 @ 1/125. K64. Tripod.

Cypress Trunks. 55mm f/3.5 Micro-Nikkor. f/8 @ 1/15. K64. Tripod.

Ferns. 55mm f/3.5 Micro-Nikkor. f/11 @ 1/15. K64. Tripod.

73-74   **Cypress Stump Planter.** 35mm f/3.5 PC Nikkor. f/8 @ 1/125. K64. Tripod.

Cypress in Fall. 105mm f/2.5 Nikkor. f/8 @ 1/60. K64.

75-76   **Sawyer's Cove.** 24mm f/2.8 Nikkor. f/11 @ 1/125. K64.

Gnarled Tree. 35mm f/3.5 PC Nikkor. f/8 @ 1/60. K64.

Fragrant Water Lily. 55mm f/3.5 Micro-Nikkor. f/11 @ 1/30. K64.

77-78   **Sunset.** 300mm f/4.5 Nikkor. f/8 @ 1/30. K64. Tripod.

Time Lapse. All three were taken from marked spot with 35mm PC Nikkor. f/11 @ 1/30. K64. Tripod.

79-80   **Spring Has Sprung.** 35mm f/3.5 PC Nikkor. f/16 @ 1/30. K64. Tripod.

Knees. 55mm f/3.5 Micro-Nikkor. f/8 @ 1/30. K64. Tripod.

Cypress Trunk. 55mm f/3.5 Micro-Nikkor. f/8 @ 1/15. K64. Tripod.

81-82   **Devil in Disguise.** 24mm f/2.8 Nikkor. f/11 @ 1/60. K64.

83-84   **Willows.** 55mm f/3.5 Micro-Nikkor. f/8 @ 1/60. K64.

Mayweed. 55mm f/3.5 Micro-Nikkor. f/16 @ 1/30. K64. Tripod.

Spider Lily. 55mm f/3.5 Micro-Nikkor. f/11 @ 1/30. K64. Tripod.

85-86   **Falling Waters.** 24mm f/2.8 Nikkor. f/11 @ 1/60. K64.

Icy Tutu. 55mm f/3.5 Micro-Nikkor. f/11 @ 1/30. K64.

Last Flight. 1000mm f/11 Reflex-Nikkor. f/11 @ 1/125. K64. Tripod.

87-88   **Yellow-top.** 55mm f/3.5 Micro-Nikkor. f/8 @ 1/125. K64.

Jakes Bayou. 55mm f/3.5 Micro-Nikkor. f/5.6 @ 1/15. K64. Tripod.

Tupelo Swamp. 55mm f/5.5 Micro-Nikkor. f/8 @ 1/60. K64.

89-90   **Cypress Island.** 105mm f/2.5 Nikkor. f/8 @ 1/250. K64. Tripod.

Cocklebur. 105mm f/4 Novoflex. f/22 @ 1/90. K64. Bellows and Strobe.

City of Knees. 24mm f/2.8 Nikkor. f/11 @ 1/125. K64. Tripod.

Notches. 55mm f/3.5 Micro-Nikkor. f/11 @ 1/30. K64. Tripod.

91-92   **Fall on the Bayou.** 55mm f/3.5 Micro-Nikkor f/8 @ 1/250. K64.

Dry Swamp. 24mm f/2.8 Nikkor. f/8 @ 1/30. K64. Tripod.

Morning Sunlight. 24mm f/2.8 Nikkor. f/8 @ 1/125. K64.

Poison Ivy. 55mm f/3.5 Micro-Nikkor. f/11 @ 1/15. K64. Tripod.

93-94   **Cypress Stump.** 105mm f/2.5 Nikkor. f/8 @ 1/250. K64.

Summer in the Swamp. 24mm f/2.8 Nikkor. f/11 @ 1/125. K64. Tripod.

Grand River Flats at Sunrise. 24mm f/2.8 Nikkor. f/11 @ 1/125. K64.

Misty Knees. 135mm f/2.8 Nikkor. f/8 @ 1/60. K64.

95-96   **Atchafalaya Morning.** 135mm f/2.8 Nikkor. f/8 @ 1/15. K64. Tripod.

Storm on the Bayou. 55mm f/3.5 Micro-Nikkor. f/11 @ four minutes. K64. Tripod.

Cypress Reflections. 35mm f/3.5 PC Nikkor. f/16 @ 1/15. K64. Tripod.

97-98   **Grand River Flats.** 35mm f/3.5 PC Nikkor. f/11 @ 1/125. K64. Tripod.

99-100   **The Dredge.** 300mm f/4.5 Nikkor. f/4.5 @ 1/125. K64. Tripod.

101-102   **Sunlight.** 24mm f/2.8 Nikkor. f/8 @ 1/125. K64.

105   **Clouds.** 55 mm f/3.5 Micro-Nikkor. f/16 @ 1/15. K64. Tripod.